What's that
BIRD?

What's that
BIRD?

Joseph DiCostanzo

**LONDON, NEW YORK, MUNICH,
MELBOURNE, AND DELHI**

DK LONDON
Senior Art Editor Jacqui Swan
Senior Editor Angeles Gavira
Editor Lizzie Munsey
US Editor Rebecca Warren
Production Editor Tony Phipps
Production Controller Nancy-Jane Maun
Jacket Designer Laura Brim
Picture Researcher Evi Peroulaki
CTS Adam Brackenbury
Managing Art Editor Michelle Baxter
Managing Editor Camilla Hallinan
Publisher Sarah Larter
Art Director Philip Ormerod
Associate Publishing Director
Liz Wheeler
Publishing Director Jonathan Metcalf

DK DELHI
Deputy Managing Art Editor
Mitun Banerjee
Managing Editor Rohan Sinha
Deputy Managing Editor
Alka Thakur Hazarika
Senior Art Editor Ivy Roy
Designers Arijit Ganguly, Arup Giri,
Pooja Pawwar, Khundongdam Rakesh
Editors Megha Gupta, Priyanka Nath
DTP Designer Bimlesh Tiwary
DTP Manager/CTS Balwant Singh
Production Manager Pankaj Sharma

First published in 2012 by DK Publishing
345 Hudson Street, New York,
New York 10014

18 19 14 13 12 11 10
026 – 178090 – Jan/2012

A catalog record for this book is available
from the Library of Congress.
ISBN 978-0-75668-968-1

DK books are available at special discounts
when purchased in bulk for sales promotions,
premiums, fund-raising, or educational use.
For details, contact: DK Publishing Special
Markets, 345 Hudson Street, New York, New
York 10014 or SpecialSales@dk.com.

Reproduced by Media Development and
Printing Ltd., UK
Printed in China

Discover more at
www.dk.com

ABOUT THE AUTHOR

Joseph DiCostanzo has been an avid birder for more than four decades. A contributor to many bird books including the AMNH's *Birds of North America* and the Smithsonian's *Birds of North America*, he has twice been president of the Linnaean Society of New York, and has been editor of the Society's newsletter for over 20 years. Joseph has also studied terns with the American Museum of Natural History's Great Gull Island Project since 1975, and has led hundreds of bird walks for the AMNH and other organizations.

Contents

Introduction

This book will help you identify the birds you see close to home and in easy-to-reach places. It provides simple profiles for the most common birds, with straightforward language and clear photos to highlight the key differences between similar-looking species. Birds are fantastic creatures. Each species is marked by distinctive shapes and colors, calls and songs. Some have different patterns and colors according to age, sex, and season. This book cannot cover all the variations, but it gives you a good start. The size, colors, and behaviors of birds make them the most accessible wild creatures for most people. Many birds live in close proximity to people. They include the world's greatest globetrotters—millions migrate thousands of miles twice a year. Living life at a fast pace, birds enjoy relatively brief, energetic lives, although some, such as fulmars (40 years) and swans (25) live longer. Birding has no rules; you just need enthusiasm, an inquiring mind, a pair of binoculars, and a notebook. So look around you and enjoy!

Joseph DiCostanzo

Identifying Birds

Learning how to identify birds requires attention to details such as shape, size, color, plumage patterns, and sound. It seems like a lot at first, but with practice, identification becomes automatic, and you will have a lot of fun as you learn. Don't expect to identify every bird—even experienced birders don't.

Size

Recognizing a bird's size might seem the simplest part of the identification process, but it can actually be one of the most difficult. The size of an individual bird without any nearby references can be deceptive. A good first step is to get a good "feel" for the size of common birds, such as the House Sparrow, American Robin, and Rock Pigeon, and then compare other birds to them. In some bird groups all species are a similar size; in others, such as these shorebirds, there is great variation, and size can be an important identifying feature.

SEMIPALMATED SANDPIPER

MARBLED GODWIT

GREATER YELLOWLEGS

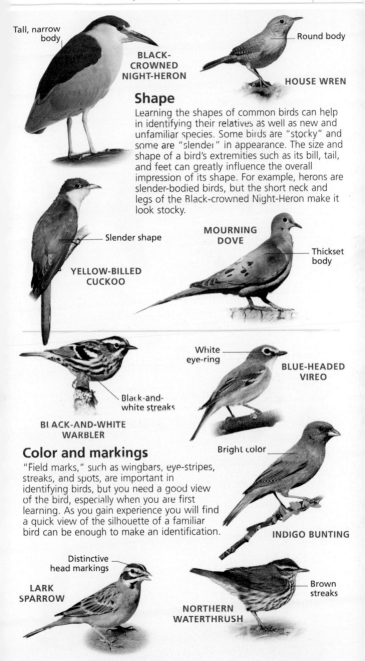

Tall, narrow body

BLACK-CROWNED NIGHT-HERON

Round body

HOUSE WREN

Shape

Learning the shapes of common birds can help in identifying their relatives as well as new and unfamiliar species. Some birds are "stocky" and some are "slender" in appearance. The size and shape of a bird's extremities such as its bill, tail, and feet can greatly influence the overall impression of its shape. For example, herons are slender-bodied birds, but the short neck and legs of the Black-crowned Night-Heron make it look stocky.

Slender shape

MOURNING DOVE

Thickset body

YELLOW-BILLED CUCKOO

White eye-ring

BLUE-HEADED VIREO

Black-and-white streaks

BLACK-AND-WHITE WARBLER

Color and markings

Bright color

"Field marks," such as wingbars, eye-stripes, streaks, and spots, are important in identifying birds, but you need a good view of the bird, especially when you are first learning. As you gain experience you will find a quick view of the silhouette of a familiar bird can be enough to make an identification.

INDIGO BUNTING

Distinctive head markings

LARK SPARROW

Brown streaks

NORTHERN WATERTHRUSH

Flight

Most birds are difficult to identify in flight, allowing only a quick glimpse as they fly past. It is easier to recognize shape and spot field marks on larger birds, especially on birds of prey, some of which spend a lot of their time circling overhead. Some birds such as swifts are never seen on the ground.

AMERICAN WOODCOCK

Long, narrow, pointed wing

GREATER YELLOWLEGS

Short, rounded wing

Long, broad, rounded wing

RED-TAILED HAWK

Rapid, blurred wings

RUFOUS HUMMINGBIRD

Wing shape

The shape of a bird's wing can help in flight identification, especially when narrowing down possibilities. Are the wings long and broad, long and narrow, short and rounded, straight or angled, flat or bowed? Some birds such as hawks can change their wing shape from broad to more stream-lined, depending on whether they are soaring or flying into the wind.

Notched

AMERICAN GOLDFINCH

MOURNING DOVE

Tail shape

Tail shape can be a great clue in identifying a flying bird. Tails can be long or short, pointed or straight, rounded, squared-off, slightly notched, or deeply forked. Some species characteristically bob or wag their tails. Wrens and Ruddy Ducks typically cock their tails upward, and many gamebirds, such as the Wild Turkey, fan them during courtship displays.

Long, pointed

RUFFED GROUSE

Rounded, fan-shaped

BARN SWALLOW

Deeply forked

Flight pattern

Size, shape, and flight action are closely linked, but some small aerial birds (such as the Chimney Swift) glide and swoop like larger species, and some big, round-winged birds (like the Ruffed Grouse) have very fast beats. Try to describe what you see: fast whirring flaps and undulations, slow flaps and floating glides, relaxed, "elastic" flaps compared with stiff, jerky beats and so on. These diagrams show some of the different flight patterns you might come across.

wingbeats

Finch-like: sequence of short, fast bursts of beats between undulating glides.

Woodpecker-like: bursts of beats between deep swoops with wings closed.

Swallow-like: sideslips and swoops with fluid, relaxed wingbeats; bursts of wingbeats between glides.

Duck-like: consistent, fast, deep wingbeats, without glides except when descending to land or water.

Sound

Most birds are extremely vocal: they call to establish territories and to keep in touch. Some birds call when they fly, and songs have sounds and patterns characteristic of a species. You hear more birds than you see (and find many by hearing them first), so learning their sounds is invaluable as well as fun. Some birds look so similar that listening to them is the best way to tell them apart.

EASTERN WHIP-POOR-WILL
Song: *whip-perrr-will,
whip-perrr will.*

LEAST FLYCATCHER
Song: *che-bek!,
che-bek!*

**WHITE-THROATED
SPARROW**
Song: *Old Sam Peabody,
Peabody, Peabody*

Range & Season

Where and when you see a bird can be an important clue in identification. Different birds have different ranges, and may not be present within these ranges at all times. Some species are resident at all times in some regions but expand their range for breeding or wintering. Other birds occur in North America only during migration between distant breeding and wintering areas.

Thrushes

These two thrushes have similar breeding ranges in summer, but the Swainson's Thrush migrates to South America, whereas the Hermit Thrush winters in the southern US.

SWAINSON'S THRUSH

HERMIT THRUSH

COMMON TERN

Terns

The Common Tern breeds in North America but spends the winter in South America. Forster's Tern is found year-round in some southern coastal areas. It also breeds in the north and winters on much of the coast.

FORSTER'S TERN

Behavior

Birds exhibit a vast variety of behaviors. Some can be helpful in identifying a bird that was only seen in a quick glimpse. Others are interesting to observe—for example, Killdeers sometimes fake a broken wing to distract attention from their nests or young. Much bird behavior can be seen in your backyard or local park.

House Wren

Though they have loud, bubbly songs, House Wrens can be shy and secretive, seeming more like a mouse in the underbrush than a bird.

Great Blue Heron

Great Blue Herons may stand motionless for long periods, waiting for fish to swim within striking distance.

Black-capped Chickadee

Chickadees are very active little birds and often form mixed feeding flocks with other small birds in winter.

Brown Creeper

Creepers search for insects in tree bark. They always start low on a tree and move upward, never downward.

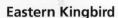

Eastern Kingbird

Kingbirds typically perch high and in the open, fly out to snatch a passing insect, and then return to their perch.

Eastern Towhee

Towhees keep their feet together as they scratch among leaf litter in the underbrush, looking for insects to eat.

Parts of Birds

Feathers are neatly arranged in particular groups called tracts. In any species, the position, size, shape, and number of feathers in each tract are remarkably consistent.

Naming the parts

Using simple terms and names for the tracts, we can write a detailed description of any bird. Here a Starling is shown perched and in flight, to show where the same feathers are in both positions. The labels on these Starlings show all you need to know to get started. Some terms are further explained in the Glossary (p.125).

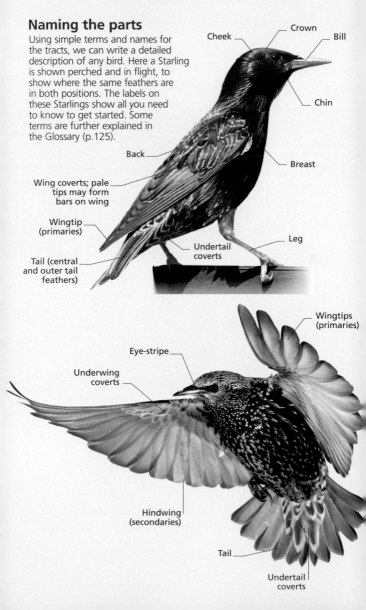

Cheek

Crown

Bill

Chin

Back

Breast

Wing coverts; pale tips may form bars on wing

Wingtip (primaries)

Undertail coverts

Leg

Tail (central and outer tail feathers)

Wingtips (primaries)

Eye-stripe

Underwing coverts

Hindwing (secondaries)

Tail

Undertail coverts

BIRD PROFILES

Starting close to home and then looking a little farther afield, these are the most common birds you can expect to see, grouped by habitat and then by appearance. Some birds can be seen in more than one habitat, but are dealt with here in the most likely one. Unless stated otherwise, where males and females look different, it is the adult male that is pictured.

Symbols

♀ Female
♂ Male
♥ Spring
☼ Summer
❄ Winter

AMERICAN ROBIN
p.30

NORTHERN CARDINAL
p.25

NORTHERN MOCKINGBIRD
p.22

Garden

Flowers, shrubs, lawns, trees, and bare earth make gardens miniature mixtures of many other habitats. Some birds thrive in this patchwork, and more can be encouraged in by food, water, and shelter provided by shrubs and trees.

1 CLOSE TO HOME

Habitats close to home are often rich and varied: don't neglect the possibilities of backyard, urban park and pond, and the nearest state park. You can learn to identify many common birds here before going farther afield to look for scarcer ones.

CANADA GOOSE
p.75

MALLARD
Male, p.64

Pond or park lake

Wild ducks and waterbirds such as Mallards, Canada Geese, coots, and several kinds of gulls easily take to suburban or even urban lakes—you never really know what might turn up next.

House

If you are lucky, you may have birds in or around the house: starlings, House Sparrows, and swifts can be seen around homes, and Barn Swallows even nest under the eaves of buildings.

BARN SWALLOW
p.29

HOUSE WREN
p.23

Town center

Even an urban or downtown area can offer a chance to see birds: Rock Pigeons or sparrows, for example, and maybe a kestrel or a Peregrine Falcon overhead. There is the possibility of a Chimney Swift or two, and maybe a Blue Jay.

ROCK PIGEON
p.27

HOUSE SPARROW
p.20

Blackbirds & Starling

These dark-colored birds often form large communal night roosts in winter. Starlings were introduced to North America from Europe in the 1890s.

EUROPEAN STARLING

Aggressive bird. In summer, adults are glossy black; young are plain gray-brown with pale throats. Fall and winter birds are heavily speckled with white, and have dark bills.

Pointed yellow bill

Black iridescent feathers

Short, square tail

RED-WINGED BLACKBIRD ♀

Similar to starling in fall and winter, but female has streaked rather than speckled plumage and shorter bill. Often has pink wash on face.

Conical bill

Pink coloring on face

Streaked plumage

♂ **see below**

RED-WINGED BLACKBIRD ♂

Medium-sized with a sharply pointed, strong bill. Prominent red shoulder patch mostly hidden on perched birds. Often found near water. Very similar Tricolored Blackbird is found only in California.

Conical bill

Black body

Red shoulder patch

♀ **see above**

What to look for • Bill shape: conical in blackbirds
• Tail length • Eye color

COMMON GRACKLE

Large, adaptable bird abundant in many habitats east of the Rockies. Iridescent purple head helps distinguish it from female Brown-headed Cowbird.

Iridescent head

Long, thick bill

Yellow eye

Long tail

BROWN-HEADED COWBIRD ♂

Widespread across North America. Males darker than females and distinguished from other blackbirds by their brown heads.

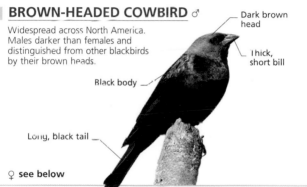

Dark brown head

Thick, short bill

Black body

Long, black tail

♀ see below

BROWN-HEADED COWBIRD ♀

Dull, pale brownish plumage; faintly streaked underparts. Does not build nests, but lays its eggs in the nests of other birds.

Plain, gray back

Short, conical bill

Pale gray underside

♂ see above

Sparrows & Finches

Except for the House Sparrow, which was introduced from Europe in the nineteenth century, these seed-eating birds are native North American species.

HOUSE SPARROW

Found in towns and cities across the continent. Female has pale eyestripe but lacks bold pattern seen on face and body of male.

Gray crown

Black and brown streaks on upperparts

Black bib

White bar on wing

Plain underparts

SONG SPARROW

One of the most common North American sparrows. Variations occur in size and shades of brown on body. Usually found in brushy areas and near water.

Gray eyebrow

Central breast spot

Rounded tail

Streaked underparts

WHITE-THROATED SPARROW

Common sparrow with distinctive whistling song. Immature has muted head stripes and blurry streaks on underside. Similar White-crowned Sparrow has grayer head and pink bill.

White or pale head stripes

Yellow patch on face

Long tail

White throat

What to look for • Bill shape and color • Color of underparts

DARK-EYED JUNCO

Widespread; eastern birds are mostly
gray while western birds have brown
backs and/or sides. All have pink bills
and white outer tails.

Gray body — — Pink bill

White outer tail — — White belly

HOUSE FINCH

Breeding male best identified by
stunning brick-red plumage—some
males are redder than others.
Female is streaked brown with no
red. Similar male Purple Finch is
unstreaked below, and western
Cassin's Finch has distinct red cap.

— Brownish cap

— Brick-red breast and head

— Heavily streaked underside

AMERICAN GOLDFINCH

Female and immature duller than bright yellow male.
Similar Lesser Goldfinch in the west has varying amounts
of black on its back, and yellow undertail feathers.

— Black cap

Black wings with
white bars —

— Unstreaked yellow body

White rump —

Mockingbirds

These birds are well known for their vocal abilities. Some string together the songs of other birds, or other sounds they hear, to make up their own varied songs.

What to look for • Wing patches • Back color

NORTHERN MOCKINGBIRD

Looks mainly gray when perched. White patches on wings and tail, distinctive in flight. Often flashes its wing patches in display.

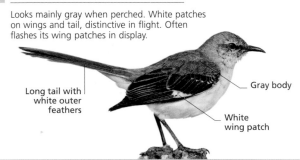

Long tail with white outer feathers

Gray body

White wing patch

GRAY CATBIRD

Named for its *mew* call, but has varied and musical songs. Often shy and retiring, but can be very conspicuous in city parks.

Blackish cap

Chestnut undertail

Slate-gray body

BROWN THRASHER

Most widespread thrasher in North America. Sometimes mimics songs of other species. Larger than western Sage Thrasher, which is grayer with a straighter bill.

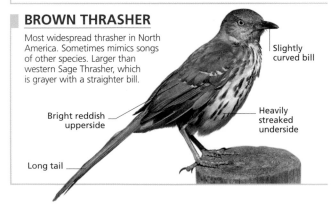

Slightly curved bill

Bright reddish upperside

Heavily streaked underside

Long tail

Small Songbirds

These tiny birds are common and widespread.
A number of wrens are limited to specialized
habitats such as canyons, deserts, and marshes.

What to look for • Face pattern • Presence of crest • Tail size

HOUSE WREN

Common backyard bird, found across the
continent. Plainest of all North American
wrens. Can be highly aggressive, driving
away nearby nesting birds.

Faint
eyebrow

Fine streaking on
wings and tail

Plain brown
body

BLACK-CAPPED CHICKADEE

Well known across the northern US and
Canada. Has distinctive black head
markings, but easiest to distinguish
by its raspy *tscik-a-dee-dee-dee* call.

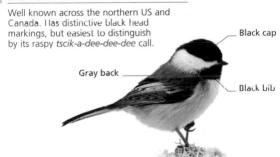

Black cap

Gray back

Black bib

TUFTED TITMOUSE

Common east of the Great Plains.
Frequent visitor to feeders, which help
it survive cold northern winters. Loud,
echoing *peter peter peter* song.

Brushy crest

Gray back

Pale brown
flanks

Woodpeckers

Woodpeckers have powerful bills, which they use for drilling into trees. Unlike other species of woodpeckers, flickers commonly feed on the ground.

What to look for • Head and back pattern

DOWNY WOODPECKER

North America's smallest and probably most common woodpecker. Found in a wide variety of wooded habitats. Similar Hairy Woodpecker is slightly larger and has a much longer bill.

White underside

White patch on back, visible in flight

White spots on black wings

RED-BELLIED WOODPECKER

The common "ladder-backed" woodpecker of the eastern US. Red on belly is rarely seen. Similar Golden-fronted Woodpecker, with yellow back of head, occurs in Texas.

Plain underside

Red crown and back of head

Black-and-white barred back

NORTHERN FLICKER

Common woodland bird found throughout North America. Underwings are yellowish in eastern birds, reddish in western birds. Similar Gilded Flicker is found in southwest desert.

Black bib

Barred brown back

Spotted underside

Bright Red Birds

These are the most common red birds in North America. Females are olive or yellow-green. Cardinals are distinguished from tanagers by their crests and thick bills.

What to look for • Bill shape and size • Presence of crest

NORTHERN CARDINAL

Familiar red bird of eastern North America. Females and young are olive or dull brown. Similar Pyrrhuloxia of Texas and the southwest is mostly gray with a red face.

Bright red back and wings

Prominent crest

Thick bill

Black face and chin

SUMMER TANAGER

Found all across the southern US. Female is olive-green, but sometimes tinged with red. Call an explosive *PIT-tuck*.

Bright red upperparts

Larger bill than Scarlet Tanager

Red wings

SCARLET TANAGER

Breeds mainly east of the Great Plains. Distinctive call, *CHIP-bruur*. Females and fall males are yellow-green with dark wings.

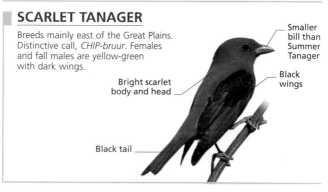

Smaller bill than Summer Tanager

Black wings

Bright scarlet body and head

Black tail

Crows

Although they look very different from each other, these three species belong to the same family. Crows are often considered among the most intelligent birds.

What to look for • Body color and pattern • Voice

BLUE JAY

Common across much of North America; found in city and suburban backyards, parks, and woodland. Loud and raucous; gives a variety of metallic-sounding calls.

Blue crest

Blue back

Black-barred tail and wings

White wing patches

AMERICAN CROW

Found in nearly all habitats. Aggressive bird, often mobs other birds in flight. Sometimes forms large winter roosts. Has a loud *caw caw* call.

Long, black bill

Black body

Tail fans out in flight

BLACK-BILLED MAGPIE

Unmistakable—in bright sunlight beautiful iridescent colors appear on its wings and tail. Abundant in the western part of the continent, but strays occur throughout.

Long tail

Black-and-white body

Blue-green sheen on wings

Pigeons & Cuckoo

Pigeons and doves are among the most familiar birds; pigeons are common even in the largest cities. Cuckoos look similar but are unrelated.

What to look for • Shape of body • Bill shape and size • Tail

ROCK PIGEON

Common city pigeon. Native to Asia, introduced around the world. Has a wide variety of plumages due to captive breeding. Wings usually have two distinctive dark bars.

Small head

Plump body

Small bill

Two bars on wing

Dark-tipped tail

MOURNING DOVE

Widespread and abundant across the continent. Found in many habitats, either perched on trees or walking on the ground.

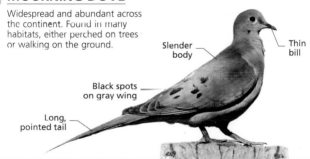

Slender body

Thin bill

Black spots on gray wing

Long, pointed tail

YELLOW-BILLED CUCKOO

Shy, slow-moving bird found in open woodland across the eastern US. Similar Black-billed Cuckoo has black bill and red eye-ring.

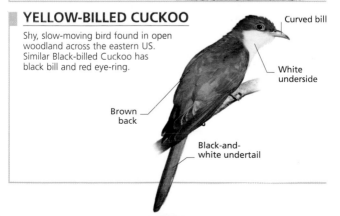

Curved bill

White underside

Brown back

Black-and-white undertail

Hummingbirds

The smallest birds in North America, hummingbirds can be mistaken for large flying insects but have distinctive long bills. Many species are restricted to the southwest.

What to look for • Throat and back color

▌RUBY-THROATED HUMMINGBIRD ♂

The most widespread hummingbird in North America, and the only one that regularly breeds east of the Great Plains. Throat can appear black at some light angles.

Long, thin bill

Iridescent red throat

Metallic green back

Dark tail, forked in flight

♀ see below

▌RUBY-THROATED HUMMINGBIRD ♀

Lacks the brightly colored throat of male. Immatures of both sexes resemble adult females. Similar Broad-tailed Hummingbird in the west has white in the outer tail.

Long, thin bill

White throat

Metallic green back

♂ see above

▌RUFOUS HUMMINGBIRD

Aggressive; drives other hummingbirds away from nectar sources. Breeding restricted to the northwest. Migrants common across much of the west; strays appear in the east in fall and winter.

Iridescent red throat

Reddish back

Reddish tail

Aerial Hunters

Swifts and swallows are sometimes mistaken for each other, but are unrelated and have very different shapes. These birds hunt for insects in the air.

What to look out for • Wing length and shape • Color of underparts

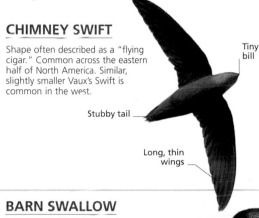

CHIMNEY SWIFT

Shape often described as a "flying cigar." Common across the eastern half of North America. Similar, slightly smaller Vaux's Swift is common in the west.

Tiny bill

Stubby tail

Long, thin wings

BARN SWALLOW

Very common everywhere, except in deserts. Named for its habit of nesting in barns; also nests in open buildings, under bridges, and other man-made structures.

Blue-black back

Reddish throat

Long, forked tail

TREE SWALLOW

Usually found near water. Often forms large flocks of thousands of birds during fall migration. Juvenile has gray-brown back.

Glossy blue-black back

White underside

Slightly notched tail

Brightly Colored Songbirds

Orioles and grosbeaks frequent the upper parts of trees; yellowthroats live on lower branches; towhees mostly on the ground; and robins are found at all levels.

AMERICAN ROBIN

The largest thrush in the US, less tied to woodland than others. Male has a darker head than female and is deeper red below; juvenile is heavily spotted black below.

Yellow bill

Gray-brown back

Brick-red underside

BALTIMORE ORIOLE

Common in the east. Females and juveniles are duller than males, with pale heads. Replaced in the west by the Bullock's Oriole, which has a large white wing patch and an orange face.

Black back and wings

White bars on wing

Orange underside

EASTERN TOWHEE

Smaller than American Robin. Scratches in leaf litter in the underbrush. Female has brown back and head. Similar to Spotted Towhee, which has white spots on its back and occurs west of the Great Plains.

Black head

Black back

Reddish sides

Long tail with white corners

What to look for • Habitat • Behavior • Bill size
• Underside color

ROSE-BREASTED GROSBEAK

Common breeder in northern woodland, migrates across the east. Female lacks the red breast of male, is brown above and streaked below, with white eyebrows.

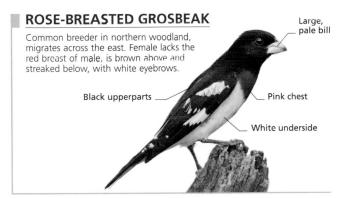

Large, pale bill

Black upperparts

Pink chest

White underside

BLACK-HEADED GROSBEAK

Western counterpart of Rose-breasted Grosbeak. Female lacks the black head of male, is brown above and cinnamon below, with white eyebrows.

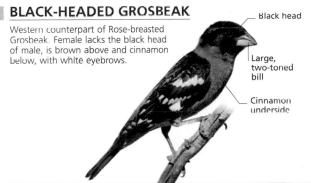

Black head

Large, two-toned bill

Cinnamon underside

COMMON YELLOWTHROAT

Usually found in low habitat, often near water or in fields and thickets. Female lacks the black mask of male; young male has a partial mask in the fall.

Greenish upperparts

Black mask

Yellow throat

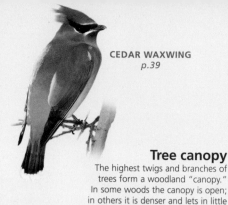

CEDAR WAXWING
p.39

Tree canopy

The highest twigs and branches of trees form a woodland "canopy." In some woods the canopy is open; in others it is denser and lets in little light. A number of birds live in the canopy, including vireos, tanagers, and some warblers.

EASTERN KINGBIRD
p.39

RED-EYED VIREO
p.44

2 WOODLAND & FOREST

Forests are home to a mixture of seed- and insect-eating birds. These include woodland specialists such as woodpeckers, nuthatches, and creepers that stay within the trees, as well as other birds like pigeons and thrushes, which also feed outside the woodland.

AMERICAN REDSTART
p.47

GOLDEN-CROWNED KINGLET
p.42

YELLOW WARBLER
p.46

Understory

Mid-height branches, shrubs, and saplings provide dense cover and good feeding opportunities for birds such as chickadees and titmice, some warblers, and kinglets. Many birds also use the forest floor to feed or nest.

Bark

Large branches and tree trunks are home to insects, insect larvae, spiders, and other invertebrates, which provide food for woodpeckers, nuthatches, and creepers. Trees also offer nest sites for birds that nest in cavities.

BROWN CREEPER
p.43

YELLOW-BELLIED SAPSUCKER
p.37

Nocturnal Hunters

These birds mainly hunt at twilight or at night. Their soft brown and gray plumage helps them remain inconspicuous during the day.

GREAT HORNED OWL

The largest owl in the US. Fierce predator, displaces even Bald Eagles from their nests. Found in forests as well as other habitats. Call is a series of deep hoots.

Large ear tufts

Large, chunky body

Barred underside

BARRED OWL

Slightly smaller than the Great Horned Owl. Common throughout the east and in far northwest. Distinctive call, a series of hoots: *who-cooks-for-you, who-cooks-for-you-all.*

Round head

Dark eyes

Barred chest

Streaked belly

EASTERN SCREECH-OWL

Like a miniature Great Horned Owl. Has two color forms: gray and bright rufous. Calls are a soft trill and a quavering whistle. Replaced in the far west by the Western Screech-Owl.

Small ear tufts

Gray or brown body

What to look for • Size • Calls • Ear tufts • Wing shape
• Throat shape • Throat color

NORTHERN PYGMY-OWL

Small owl of western woodland.
Hunts during the day—unlike the
slightly larger, and strictly nocturnal
Northern Saw-whet Owl—but is
most active at twilight. Call is a
whistled series of *hoo* notes.

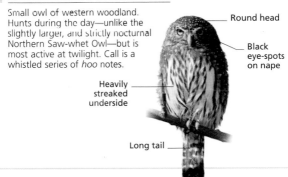

Round head

Black
eye-spots
on nape

Heavily
streaked
underside

Long tail

COMMON NIGHTHAWK

Found in summer across the continent,
except in the southwest. Most active at
dawn and dusk, when it hunts flying
insects. Male has white throat; female has
grayish brown throat. Call is a nasal *peent*.

Very
small bill

Long, pointed
wings

Long,
slightly
forked tail

White
wing patch

EASTERN WHIP-POOR-WILL

More nocturnal than nighthawks, with
shorter, less pointed wings. Male has
black throat, white collar; female
has brown throat, pale collar. Named
for its distinctive call, *whip-perrr-wiil*.

Wide,
flat bill

Black throat

Rounded
wings

Rounded
tail

Gamebirds

These small to large gamebirds are easy to identify, although there are some gamebirds and related species in the west and far north that could cause confusion.

What to look for • Size • Face pattern

RUFFED GROUSE

Medium-sized grouse. Only the male has the dark "ruff" that gives the bird its name. Males make a deep, drumming noise with their wings as part of their territorial display.

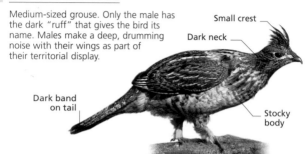

Small crest

Dark neck

Dark band on tail

Stocky body

NORTHERN BOBWHITE

Quail, about half the size of Ruffed Grouse. Female has a brownish throat and an eye-stripe. Occurs in brush areas and woodland in the eastern US. Call is a loud, whistled *bob-white*.

Small head

White throat

Plump body

Short tail

WILD TURKEY

Unmistakable due to its unusual shape and size. Twice as large as a grouse, though a strong flier. Often roosts in trees. Increasing in number in many areas.

Small head

Tail fanned in display

Iridescent feathers

Woodpeckers

Woodpeckers are easy to recognize due to their strong bills and their habit of clinging upright to tree trunks and limbs.

What to look for • Size • Face pattern

RED-HEADED WOODPECKER

Medium-sized, with a very distinctive red head. Juveniles have a brown head and brown-barred back. Frequents open woodlands, orchards, and forests.

Red head

White underside

Black back

White wing patch

YELLOW-BELLIED SAPSUCKER

Medium-sized woodpecker. Breeds across northern forests, winters in southern forests. Similar-looking Red-naped Sapsucker is common in the west and has a red patch on the back of its head.

Black chest

Red forehead

White wing patch

PILEATED WOODPECKER

As large as a crow and nearly twice the size of any other North American woodpecker. Large white wing lining visible in flight. Female has a black forehead.

Red crest

Black back

Black wings

Flycatchers & Waxwing

These are small to medium-sized migrant songbirds that perch in an upright posture. Flycatchers race after flying insects, whereas waxwings feed on berries.

EASTERN PHOEBE

Common breeder across eastern US. Resident in mid-south; winters in southeast. Frequently occurs near water. Song a distinctive *FEE-bee*.

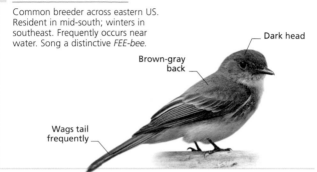

Dark head

Brown-gray back

Wags tail frequently

EASTERN WOOD-PEWEE

Uniform head and back color help distinguish it from Eastern Phoebe. Song a whistled *pee-wee, pee-wee*, sometimes followed by *pee-urr*. Replaced in the west by Western Wood-Pewee.

Gray-olive back

Pale lower bill

Faint bars on wings

Pale belly

LEAST FLYCATCHER

Smallest eastern flycatcher. One of 11 very similar small flycatchers, six of which are restricted to the west. Best identified by emphatic *che-bek song*.

White eye-ring

Olive-green back

White bars on wing

What to look for • Size • Voice • Bars on wings • Back and head color • Color of underparts

EASTERN KINGBIRD

Larger than most flycatchers. Conspicuous, usually perching in the open, often near water. Western Kingbird (p.52) has a yellow belly.

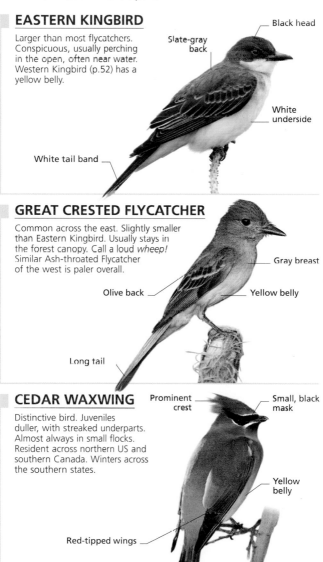

Black head

Slate-gray back

White underside

White tail band

GREAT CRESTED FLYCATCHER

Common across the east. Slightly smaller than Eastern Kingbird. Usually stays in the forest canopy. Call a loud *wheep!* Similar Ash-throated Flycatcher of the west is paler overall.

Gray breast

Olive back

Yellow belly

Long tail

CEDAR WAXWING

Distinctive bird. Juveniles duller, with streaked underparts. Almost always in small flocks. Resident across northern US and southern Canada. Winters across the southern states.

Prominent crest

Small, black mask

Yellow belly

Red-tipped wings

Thrushes & Blue Birds

These brown thrushes are all migrants to North America. The Eastern Bluebird is also a thrush, but the other two blue birds are finches, with thick bills.

VEERY

Common breeder in dense forests in the northern US and southern Canada. Uniform brown back. Larger Wood Thrush has a bright brown crown, spotted chest, and breeds exclusively in the east.

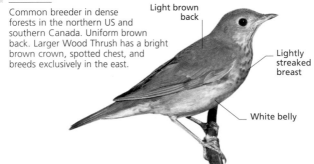

Light brown back

Lightly streaked breast

White belly

HERMIT THRUSH

Smallest and most widespread of the brown thrushes. Often seen in wooded areas in urban and suburban parks. The only thrush to winter in the US.

Reddish brown tail, frequently pumped up and down

Whitish eye-ring

Heavily streaked throat

SWAINSON'S THRUSH

Breeds from Alaska to eastern Canada, and in western and eastern mountains; migrant everywhere else. Buffy eye-ring helps distinguish it from similar Gray-cheeked Thrush.

Olive-brown back

Buff-colored eye-ring

Pale, streaked chest

What to look for • Back color and pattern • Eye-ring
• Bars on wings • Throat color

EASTERN BLUEBIRD

Partial migrant; resident in much
of the east. Female duller than
male, with gray blue upperparts. In
the west, similar Western Bluebird
has blue throat, and Mountain
Bluebird is sky blue.

Bright
blue back

Reddish
throat
and
chest

White belly

INDIGO BUNTING

Male is smallest all-blue bird; female is
plain brown. Breeds in eastern and central
part of the continent. In the west, Lazuli
Bunting has cinnamon breast and white
bars on wings.

Small,
thick bill

Blue body

BLUE GROSBEAK

Larger than Indigo Bunting, with
much larger bill. Prefers woodland
edges and brushy areas. Female is
plain brown, with chestnut bars
on wings.

Thick bill

Chestnut
bars on wing

Blue body

Tiny Songbirds

These are among the smallest birds in North America; only hummingbirds are smaller. Their songs range from short notes and nasal wheezes to loud, clear notes.

What to look for • Tail length and color • Back color

BLUE-GRAY GNATCATCHER

Like a tiny Northern Mockingbird (p.22). Only male has black line over eye. Resident in southeast and southern California; summer breeder in much of the rest of the US.

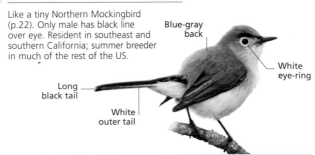

Blue-gray back

White eye-ring

Long black tail

White outer tail

BUSHTIT

Usually gathers in flocks. Resident in parts of the west. Variable plumage: ear patches are brown on inland birds, black on some southwestern birds, and coastal birds have a brown crown.

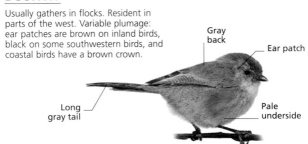

Gray back

Ear patch

Long gray tail

Pale underside

GOLDEN-CROWNED KINGLET

Resident at high elevations in east and west US. Breeds in coniferous forest in northern Canada; migrates and winters across the US. Similar Ruby-crowned Kinglet has a white eye-ring.

Golden crown

White eye-line

Small bill

Broken bars on wing

Tree Creepers

Although they are unrelated, these birds share the unusual habit of creeping along tree trunks and branches in search of insects.

What to look for • Shape • Back color and pattern
• Bill shape

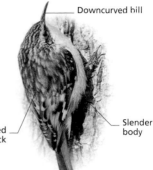

Downcurved bill

BROWN CREEPER

Looks like a moving piece of tree bark; streaked brown back is camouflaged against tree trunks. Moves up main trunk of a tree, then flies down to start up another tree.

Streaked
brown back

Slender
body

WHITE-BREASTED NUTHATCH

The largest nuthatch. Resident throughout the continent. Moves up and down tree trunks and branches. Similar, widespread Red-breasted Nuthatch is smaller and has a white eye line.

Slate-
gray
back

Black cap

Pointed
bill

Plump
body

BLACK-AND-WHITE WARBLER

Similar in size to Brown Creeper. Females and immatures have white throats; males have black throats. A common breeder and migrant in east and central US.

Striped
back

Striped
head

Black streaks
underneath

Vireos

These small, yellow-green birds are sometimes confused with warblers due to their similar size. However, they have thicker bills than warblers and are less active.

What to look for • Bars on wings • "Spectacles" • Eye-lines

RED-EYED VIREO

Long, slender bird with deep red eyes. Common summer breeder, except in the west, where it is a rare migrant. Song a series of short, whistled phrases.

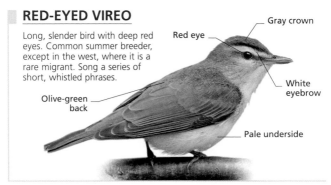

Red eye

Gray crown

White eyebrow

Olive-green back

Pale underside

WARBLING VIREO

A nondescript, dull bird. Migrant; breeds across the continent. Sings a long, complex song, often while sitting immobile, hidden in mid- to upper canopy.

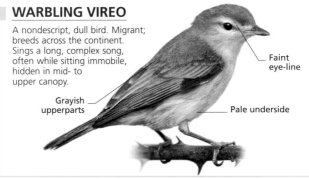

Faint eye-line

Grayish upperparts

Pale underside

BLUE-HEADED VIREO

Gray head, white throat, and "spectacles." Breeds across much of Canada and higher elevations in the east; winters in southern states.

Slate-blue head

White "spectacles"

Olive back

Yellow sides

Dull Warblers

Over 40 species of warblers breed in North America. All are migrants, and only one or two species winter on the continent. These are some of the less colorful warblers.

What to look for • Streaks underneath • Stripes on head

ORANGE-CROWNED WARBLER

One of the plainest warblers, with rather dull plumage. Breeds across the high Arctic and in the west; uncommon winter migrant in the east.

Olive back

Faint eye-line

Yellow undertail

Faint streaks underneath

OVENBIRD

An unusual warbler. Common breeder and migrant over eastern two-thirds of the continent. Walks stealthily on forest floor. Song a loud *teacher, teacher, teacher.*

Reddish crown stripe

White eye-ring

Olive back

Streaked underside

NORTHERN WATERTHRUSH

Common breeder in wet, wooded areas across northern North America. Walks on ground. Similar-looking Louisiana Waterthrush in the east has pinker legs and bolder, whiter eyebrows.

Dark olive-green back

Prominent eyebrow

Bobs tail

Streaked underside

Bright Warblers

These active, insect-eating birds are usually found in the mid- to upper canopy. They are mainly yellow, dull green, blue, and red in color.

YELLOW WARBLER

One of the most common warblers. Favors open woodland near water. Female less bright than male, with fewer breast streaks. Juvenile birds are duller.

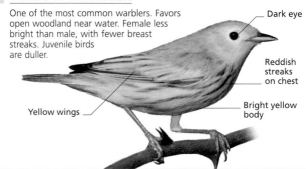

Dark eye

Reddish streaks on chest

Bright yellow body

Yellow wings

BLUE-WINGED WARBLER

Bright yellow warbler with blue-gray wings. Female duller than male. Relatively common breeder and migrant in the east. Typical *beee-bzzzz* song, with the second part softer than the first.

Black eyestripe

White bars on wing

Blue-gray wings

Bright yellow underside

WILSON'S WARBLER

Mostly olive-colored warbler with a black cap. Breeds across northern North America; migrant everywhere, but more common in west. Prefers lower thickets and tangles.

Black cap

Olive back

Olive wings

Bright yellow underside

What to look for • Face pattern • Wing bars and patches
• Underside color • Streaks on back and chest

YELLOW-RUMPED WARBLER

Abundant; breeds across Canada and
higher elevations in east and west, winters
in southern states. Western birds have
yellow throats. Female has brown streaks
on back.

Streaks on back
and chest

Yellow rump

Yellow
sides of
chest

MAGNOLIA WARBLER

Breeds in much of Canada. Common
migrant in east US, rarer in west.
Female has streaked green back
and fewer breast streaks than male.
Bars on wing are larger than on
Blue-winged Warbler.

White
bars on
wing

Black
streaks
on chest

Yellow
underside

White band
on tail

AMERICAN REDSTART

Common breeder across north and
in the east; uncommon migrant in
west. Females and immatures have
gray-green backs with yellow wing
and tail patches.

Orange
wing
patch

Orange
sides

White belly

Orange tail
patch

3 OPEN COUNTRY

Modern, efficient farming means fewer opportunities for birds in the countryside, because there are fewer seeds and insects available for them to eat. However, grassland, field margins, and farms all offer habitats for different birds.

HORNED LARK
p.54

UPLAND SANDPIPER
p.50

KILLDEER
p.50

Open meadow

Grassland birds include larks, pipits, starlings, crows, and meadowlarks, which need insects, seeds, and worms at different times of year. Most feed their chicks high-nutrient insect food.

WESTERN MEADOWLARK
p.55

Skies

The open air should
not be neglected as
a habitat—swifts
and swallows feed
exclusively in the
air, often over open
farmland or wetlands,
and vultures and
hawks use the sky as
a viewpoint from which
to see prey.

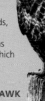

RED-TAILED HAWK
p.57

Hedges and thickets

Good hedges and thickets have many
berries, which are ideal for birds to eat in
late summer, fall, and early winter. They
are also great hunting grounds for birds
such as shrikes, and provide cover for
others, such as sparrows.

**LARK
SPARROW**
p.53

**LOGGERHEAD
SHRIKE**
p.53

SAY'S PHEOBE
p.52

**WESTERN
KINGBIRD**
p.52

Ground Birds

These birds should be looked for on shores, in open fields and grasslands, or in very open, dry habitats.

KILLDEER

The most common and widespread plover. Resident all year round in the southern US; may breed anywhere that has open ground, except in the high Arctic.

Gray-brown back

Double breast band

White underside

UPLAND SANDPIPER

Medium-sized, migrant sandpiper. Rarely found on the shore; breeds in grasslands and open fields from the east to the Great Plains and the high prairies.

Small head

Large, dark eye

Plump body

GREATER ROADRUNNER

A terrestrial cuckoo, completely unlike other members of its family. Unmistakable due to its large crest and long, dark tail. Found in dry, open habitats in the southwest from Arkansas to California.

Large bill

Long tail

Streaked brown body

What to look for • Size • Shape • Breast and belly markings • Behavior

SHORT-EARED OWL

Flies like giant moth. Can be found across the continent in winter. Hunts over open country, particularly at twilight. Roosts on ground or low structures in the day.

Very small ear tufts

Black "wrist" marks on wing, visible in flight

Streaked underneath

BURROWING OWL

Nests in burrows in the ground. Hunts at night; stands upright in front of burrow or on posts during day. Main range is west of the Great Plains; isolated Florida population.

Yellow eyes

Brown upperparts with white spots

Long legs

GREATER SAGE-GROUSE

Large, distinctive bird of western sagebrush. Spectacular black-and-white pattern. In display, male inflates air sacs on throat and chest. Female lacks air sacs and spiky tail.

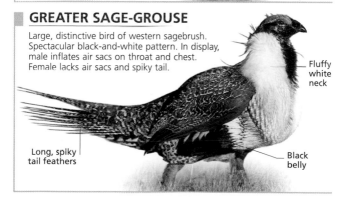

Fluffy white neck

Long, spiky tail feathers

Black belly

Flycatchers & Finch

Unlike many other flycatchers, this kingbird and phoebe frequent open spaces. The Dickcissel prefers open grasslands and unmown roadsides.

What to look out for • Color of underparts • Bill shape and color

WESTERN KINGBIRD

Common breeder from the Great Plains westward. Perches on wires and fences. Migrant; strays throughout the east. Very similar Cassin's Kingbird has dark gray head and back.

Gray head

Gray back

White outer tail edge

Black tail

Yellow belly

SAY'S PHOEBE

Smaller than Western Kingbird. Common breeder in dry areas in the west from Alaska to the Mexican border. Migrant; strays can appear anywhere in the east.

Dark head

Gray-brown back

Tawny belly

DICKCISSEL ♂

Slightly smaller than Say's Phoebe. Common breeder in central US; rarely as far as the east coast. Forms large flocks during migration; strays can occur anywhere in North America.

Yellow eyebrow

Black bib

Yellow chest

Chestnut shoulder patch

Sparrows & Shrike

Many sparrows are small brown birds, but Chipping and Lark Sparrows are well patterned. Shrikes are predatory songbirds, which often impale their prey on thorns.

What to look for • Shape • Size • Head and face pattern

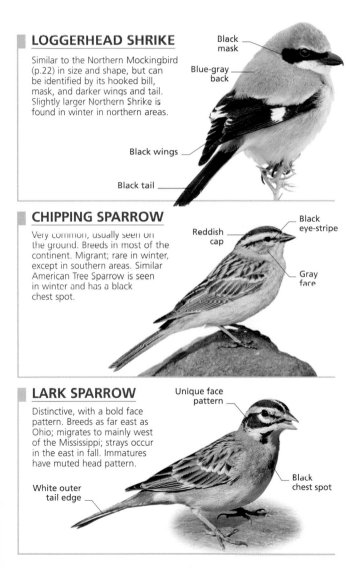

LOGGERHEAD SHRIKE

Similar to the Northern Mockingbird (p.22) in size and shape, but can be identified by its hooked bill, mask, and darker wings and tail. Slightly larger Northern Shrike is found in winter in northern areas.

Black mask

Blue-gray back

Black wings

Black tail

CHIPPING SPARROW

Very common, usually seen on the ground. Breeds in most of the continent. Migrant; rare in winter, except in southern areas. Similar American Tree Sparrow is seen in winter and has a black chest spot.

Reddish cap

Black eye-stripe

Gray face

LARK SPARROW

Distinctive, with a bold face pattern. Breeds as far east as Ohio; migrates to mainly west of the Mississippi; strays occur in the east in fall. Immatures have muted head pattern.

Unique face pattern

Black chest spot

White outer tail edge

Winter Flocking Birds

These sparrow-sized birds gather in mixed flocks in winter. They share an upright posture and white in the tail but are from different families.

What to look for • Face and head patern • Back color • Bill shape

AMERICAN PIPIT

Highly migratory; breeds on Arctic tundra and western mountaintops; winters across southern portion of the continent. Often pumps its tail up and down.

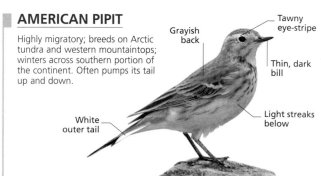

Grayish back

Tawny eye-stripe

Thin, dark bill

Light streaks below

White outer tail

HORNED LARK

Distinctive, with tiny "horns" on head. Resident across the US; birds breeding in Canada and Alaska mostly retreat south in the winter months.

Unique head pattern

Yellowish face

White outer tail

SNOW BUNTING

Highly migratory; breeds in much of Alaska and in the high Arctic. Winters across southern Canada and the northern US. Breeding male has black back and bill.

Chestnut crown

White wing patch

White outer tail

Distinctive Blackbirds

These blackbirds are boldly patterned. The Yellow-headed Blackbird breeds in wet areas, but often feeds in farmland; the other two prefer grasslands.

What to look for • Head color and pattern • White patches on wings

YELLOW-HEADED BLACKBIRD

Male unmistakable, with bright yellow head. Female and immature much duller than male. Common breeder in parts of the west, less common in Midwest; strays occur in the east on fall migration and in winter.

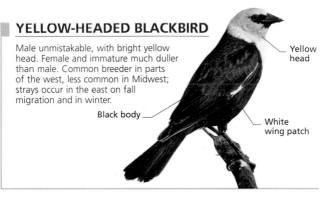

Yellow head

Black body

White wing patch

BOBOLINK

Plumage of breeding male unmistakable. Females and fall birds are brown, with streaked backs and brown-striped heads. Migrant; breeds across southern Canada and northern US.

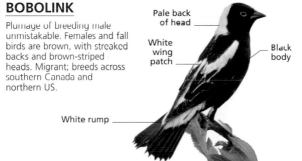

Pale back of head

White wing patch

Black body

White rump

WESTERN MEADOWLARK

Common in the west. Gathers in flocks in winter. Male and female look alike; no marked difference between summer and winter plumage. Eastern Meadowlark is very similar.

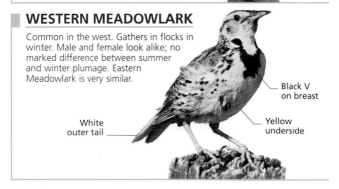

Black V on breast

White outer tail

Yellow underside

Vultures, Eagles, & Hawks

This group of birds generally has broad wings and spends much time soaring. Vultures can be confused with hawks in the air.

TURKEY VULTURE

Common nearly everywhere in summer; winters mainly in the south. Soars with wings held in shallow "V." Flight feathers are silvery underneath. Similar Black Vulture has white patches on wings, visible in flight.

Bare, red head

Black body

BALD EAGLE

Population increasing across the US. Immature is all brown with blotchy white on underside and especially underwings. Adult has white head, white tail, and no white anywhere else. Similar Golden Eagle, found mainly in the western US, is darker; immature has white tail base.

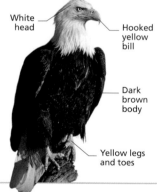

White head

Hooked yellow bill

Dark brown body

Yellow legs and toes

OSPREY

Catches fish by hovering over water and then diving feet first. In flight, prominent dark "wrist" marks are visible on its long wings, which are bent backward at "wrist." Winters in South America.

White head

Dark eye-stripe

Dark brown back

Speckled chest

White belly

What to look for • Underside and underwing color
• Wing marks • Flight style

RED-TAILED HAWK

Common resident throughout
most of the continent; soars over
many habitats. Immature has dark,
banded tail. Has both paler and
darker color forms in the west.

White spots
on back

Streaks on
belly

Red tail

BROAD-WINGED HAWK

Common in summer throughout the
east; sometimes migrates in large
flocks during fall. In flight, underside
of wings has a dark outline. Faint
bars on tail on immature (pictured)
turn to bands in adult.

Brown spots
on underside of
juvenile, reddish
bars on adult

Barred tail

SWAINSON'S HAWK

Primarily occurs in the west; strays to the east
on migration. Often migrates in large flocks.
Dark and light (pictured) color forms occur.

Dark brown
back

Pale
reddish
breast

Barred tail

Pointed-winged Birds of Prey

These birds rarely soar except when migrating. Falcons and kites have relatively long, pointed wings and can reach high speeds during dives.

WHITE-TAILED KITE

Mainly found in the south and the west; strays occur over most of the US. Immatures have rufous streaks on head and undersides. Similar Mississippi Kite has dark tail.

Black shoulder

White underside

Gray above

Whitish tail

NORTHERN HARRIER

Found across the continent. Flies low, back and forth over marshes and grasslands, with wings held upward. Females brown-backed and streaked below; immatures have cinnamon undersides.

Facial disk

Long wings

White rump, obvious in flight

COOPER'S HAWK

Resident in woodlands throughout North America, except in the far north. Immatures brown-backed and streaked below. Similar Sharp-shinned Hawk is slightly smaller, with squared-off tail and small head.

Dark cap

Short, rounded wings

Long, rounded tail

What to look for • Wing shape • Face pattern • Tail and rump color

AMERICAN KESTREL

Smallest North American falcon, common across the continent. Nests in cities and open country; hovers while hunting. Females and immatures have brown backs and brown streaks below.

Rusty back

Two black face stripes

Long, pointed wings

MERLIN

Mid-sized dark falcon with heavily streaked underside. Breeds across Canada and mountainous areas in the west; winters mainly in the west and the extreme south. Migrants found in a variety of habitats.

Dark back

Long, pointed wings

Dark tail

PEREGRINE FALCON

Large falcon. Breeds mainly in the Arctic and in mountains in the west. Has been reestablished in the east, where it nests on buildings, bridges, and other man-made structures. Immatures have brown backs.

Dark crown

Large, dark "mustache"

Dark back

Horizontal barring on underside

Birds of Prey

Birds of prey vary in size, from the small kestrel to large eagles. The larger species soar on warm air currents while hunting or migrating, saving a lot of energy.

Identifying birds in flight can be difficult. It is hard to judge the size of an individual in the sky, and colors can be difficult to see when a bird is in silhouette. The proportions of the bird, the shape and size of its wings, tail, and head, and the style of flight can all be important in identification.

What to look for

• Wing shape: broad or narrow, long or short?

• Wingtip shape: pointed or fanned?

• Tail: closed or fanned, square or rounded, notched or forked?

• Head: large and protruding, small with little visible neck?

• Flight: "lazy" with few wingbeats, or active with a lot of flapping?

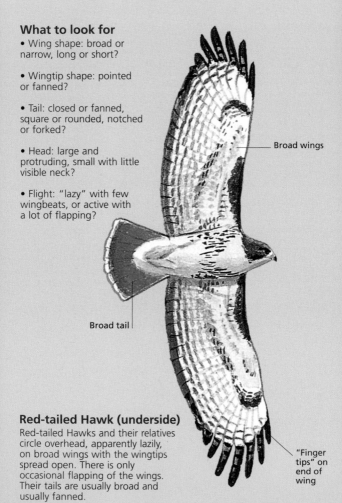

Broad wings

Broad tail

"Finger tips" on end of wing

Red-tailed Hawk (underside)

Red-tailed Hawks and their relatives circle overhead, apparently lazily, on broad wings with the wingtips spread open. There is only occasional flapping of the wings. Their tails are usually broad and usually fanned.

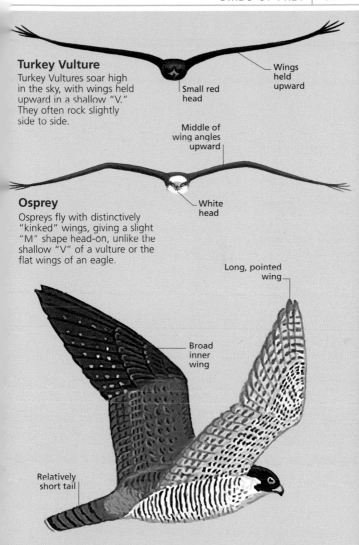

Turkey Vulture

Turkey Vultures soar high in the sky, with wings held upward in a shallow "V." They often rock slightly side to side.

Wings held upward

Small red head

Middle of wing angles upward

Osprey

Ospreys fly with distinctively "kinked" wings, giving a slight "M" shape head-on, unlike the shallow "V" of a vulture or the flat wings of an eagle.

White head

Long, pointed wing

Broad inner wing

Relatively short tail

Peregrine Falcon (upperside)

Peregrine Falcons have powerful, streamlined wings built for fast flight. In a dive or "stoop" they can reach speeds of 200 miles per hour. Peregrines will also sometimes soar on updrafts like other hawks.

SHORT-BILLED DOWITCHER
p.88

BLACK-BELLIED PLOVER
Summer, p.86

Open shore

Wading birds find food on or within mud, sand, and silt, or in shallow water. Some birds sieve water for seeds and minute animal matter; others probe the mud for worms, or hunt fish and frogs.

GREAT BLUE HERON
p.80

4 WATER & WATERSIDE

Water adds great variety to the habitats and food in a landscape, and increases the number and variety of birds. If water is near woodland or open ground, the landscape will be especially rich in wildlife.

BLACK-CROWNED NIGHT-HERON
p.80

GADWALL
Female, p.66

COMMON LOON
Summer, p.76

On the water

Some birds use open water as a safe place to sleep or rest. Others feed there, finding floating seeds and insects, or diving underwater to find fish, invertebrates such as shellfish, or plants.

Reeds and sedges

Many water birds are secretive and need dense vegetation to feed or nest in; others come to these areas to roost at night. Winter or summer, reedy areas alongside water are always worth a long, close look.

COMMON GALLINULE
p.78

GREEN HERON
p.81

VIRGINIA RAIL
p.78

Male Dabbling Ducks

Sometimes called "puddle ducks," these dabblers rarely dive, but tip up to feed with their heads underwater and tails in the air. They favor freshwater habitats.

WOOD DUCK ♂

Small and unmistakable, with bright plumage and drooping crest, which gives it a helmet-like profile. Partially migratory. In summer, breeds southward from southern Canada, except in drier areas of the west.

Distinctive face pattern

Drooping crest

Brown chest with white stripes on sides

♀ **p.66**

MALLARD ♂

The most familiar duck; back varies from gray to gray-brown. Abundant and resident over much of the continent. In summer, breeds north to the high Arctic; northern birds migrate south in winter.

Metallic green head

Gray-brown body

White collar

Brown chest

♀ **p.66**

GADWALL ♂

Slightly smaller than Mallard. Partially migratory; in winter is found over much of central and southern states. Breeds in central regions and into Canada. Resident in far west.

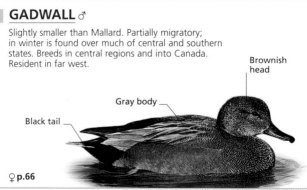

Brownish head

Gray body

Black tail

♀ **p.66**

What to look for • Head color and pattern • Size
• Color on sides • Color of tail feathers

GREEN-WINGED TEAL ♂

Smallest puddle duck in North America;
fairly common. Migratory; breeds in Alaska,
across Canada, and in northern states.
Winters throughout the south. Resident
in the northwest.

Green ear patch

Chestnut head

Vertical white
stripe on sides
of chest

♀ **p.67**

AMERICAN WIGEON ♂

Slightly smaller than Gadwall. In flight, shows
large white wing patch on upperwing and
white wing lining underneath. Migratory;
distribution similar to Green-winged Teal.

Pale
head

Green ear
patch

Black
under
tail

Brown
sides and
chest

♀ **p.67**

NORTHERN PINTAIL ♂

Largest of North American puddle ducks, long
tail makes it appear even bigger. Migratory;
distribution similar to American Wigeon
and Green-winged Teal.

Brown
head

Long, pointed
central tail
feathers

Long neck

White
chest

♀ **p.67**

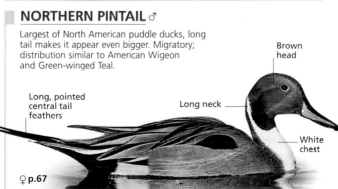

Female Dabbling Ducks

Female dabbling ducks are usually much plainer, and mostly browner or grayer than the males. In summer, males molt and look more like females.

◼ WOOD DUCK ♀

Breeds in woodland near water; nests in tree cavities and in nest boxes. Juveniles resemble females.

Gray-brown back

Short, drooping crest

Distinctive eye-patch

Blue wing patch

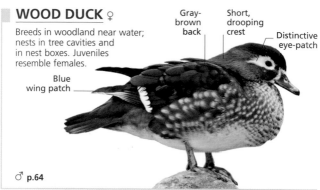

♂ **p.64**

◼ MALLARD ♀

Fairly plain, brown duck with blue wing patch; head paler than body, as with other female dabblers. In the east, similar American Black Duck's body is much darker than its head.

Pale head

Mottled brown body

Orange and black bill

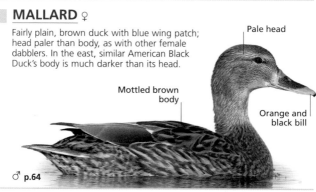

♂ **p.64**

◼ GADWALL ♀

Easily confused with female Mallard, but is slightly smaller, has white on wing and belly, and more orange on sides of bill.

Dark eye-stripe

Dark upper bill

White wing patch

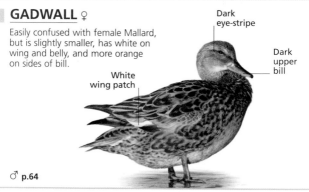

♂ **p.64**

What to look for • Size • Shape • Color of wing patch • Color of belly

GREEN-WINGED TEAL ♀

Very small, mottled brown duck. Easily confused with female Blue-winged and Cinnamon teals, but can be identified by its much smaller bill and green wing patch.

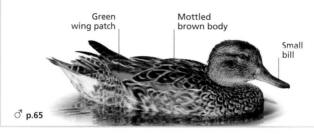

Green wing patch

Mottled brown body

Small bill

♂ **p.65**

AMERICAN WIGEON ♀

Resembles male, unlike many female ducks, but all colors and patterns are more muted. Also lacks green ear patch of male.

Grayish head

Dark smudge around eye

Brown chest and sides

♂ **p.65**

NORTHERN PINTAIL ♀

Easily distinguished from other female ducks by its size and shape, particularly its long neck and tail.

Gray bill

Long neck

Pointed tail

♂ **p.65**

Male Diving Ducks

These ducks dive completely underwater when feeding, rather than tipping up. The Northern Shoveler is a dabbling duck, and the lone exception.

NORTHERN SHOVELER ♂

Common, medium-sized dabbler with a distinctive long bill. Most breed from Alaska to the Great Plains; scattered breeders occur eastward. Winters in the south and on the coast.

Green head

Large "shovel" bill

Rusty brown sides

White chest

♀ p.70

REDHEAD ♂

Upper parts and flanks appear gray, but show fine black markings close up. Migratory. Primarily breeds in the west; winters in south and at the coasts.

Reddish head

Gray back

Gray sides

Black breast

♀ p.70

LESSER SCAUP ♂

Most common diving duck in North America. Migratory; breeds in Alaska, Canada, and some northern and western states; winters throughout much of the US. Greater Scaup is similar but larger, with a rounder head.

Pointed crown

Dark head

Gray back

Black chest

♀ p.70

What to look for • Head color and pattern • Bill shape • Size

BUFFLEHEAD ♂

Very small, distinctive, large-headed duck. Migratory; breeds in the north; winters on the coast and across much of the US. Usually nests in abandoned tree cavities.

White head patch

Black forehead

Black back

White underside

♀ **p.71**

COMMON MERGANSER ♂

Large waterbird, nearly twice the size of the Bufflehead. Eats mostly fish. Found across the continent, but rarely frequents salt water.

Dark head

Thin, red bill

Dark back

♀ **p.71**

RUDDY DUCK ♂

Small duck, slightly larger than the Bufflehead. Non-breeding males resemble females, but have black rather than blue bills. Both sexes hold their tails in "cocked" position.

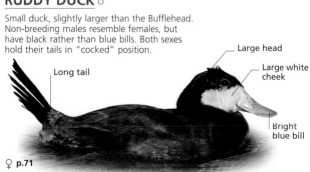

Large head

Large white cheek

Long tail

Bright blue bill

♀ **p.71**

Female Diving Ducks

Female diving ducks are much plainer than males, in the same way as female dabblers. Often the best way to tell them apart is by identifying the accompanying male.

NORTHERN SHOVELER ♀

Medium-sized duck with unique bill shape and greenish wing patch which is visible in flight. Both sexes have distinctive feeding behavior—they often form rotating circles of birds and use their bills to strain the water for food.

Large, shovel-like bill

Brown overall

♂ **p.68**

REDHEAD ♀

Medium-sized, brown bird; perhaps the plainest of all North American ducks. Best identified by gray bill with black tip.

Dark crown

Black bill tip

Brown back

Pale throat

♂ **p.68**

LESSER SCAUP ♀

Smaller than Redhead. In winter, favors freshwater habitats more than larger, extremely similar-looking Greater Scaup.

Dark brown head

White behind bill

Brown back and chest

♂ **p.68**

What to look for • Size • Bill shape • Head pattern

BUFFLEHEAD ♀

The smallest diving duck in North America.
Unlikely to be confused with any duck,
except for slightly larger Ruddy Duck.

Black head

White
ear patch

Dark, unmarked back

Pale underside

♂ p.69

COMMON MERGANSER ♀

Long, slender, and very clean-looking
duck. Sharp division between its
chestnut-colored neck and
whitish breast.

Chestnut
head

Red
bill

Gray body

Distinct
white
chin

♂ p.69

RUDDY DUCK ♀

Small and squat-looking, with dusky line
running through whitish cheek. Tail
often raised. Overall appearance unlike
that of any other duck.

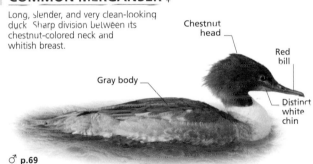

Dark crown

Whitish cheek

Stubby
tail

♂ p.69

Ducks

Duck plumage varies depending on age, sex, and season. Breeding male, summer male, female, and juvenile birds can look quite different.

Duck "breeding" plumages are at their best through winter and spring. In summer they molt their flight feathers and cannot fly. Males molt to a dull "eclipse" plumage for the summer—at this time of year, camouflage is more important than splendid color.

Mallards

Even the common, tame Mallards of park lakes are worth studying closely. Although males and females share a basic size and shape, they look different, and the male plumage changes with the seasons.

White tail

Blue wing patch

Orange-and-black bill

Curly tail

Female

Mallard females are brown all year around but can be identified by features such as the bright blue wing patch (speculum), white tail, and leg and bill colors.

Ruddy Ducks

Large heads, chunky bodies, and large tails give these small ducks a distinctive appearance. They and their relatives are called "stifftails" because of their spiky tails, which are often held upright. Ruddy Ducks often gather in large flocks on enclosed bodies of water such as ponds and bays. They feed by diving completely underwater.

Female

Female Ruddy Ducks are darker overall than the males. They can always be distinguished from the males by the single line through their dusky cheek.

Dusky cheek

Head turns red-brown but in-between stages are common

Yellow beak

Summer male

Males in "eclipse" plumage look similar to females, but have redder feathers and yellow beaks. This male is halfway between eclipse and full breeding colors.

Winter male

Bright male Mallards in breeding plumage can be seen from late fall to early spring. Their feathers are glossy and immaculate.

Green head

Yellow beak

White collar

Winter male

Unlike most other ducks, male Ruddy Ducks spend most of the winter in a dull non-breeding plumage. However, they are always brighter than females.

Rusty body

White cheek

Summer male

In the early spring, male Ruddy Ducks bills turn bright blue, and their backs and bodies become a bright, rusty brown.

Large Waterfowl

Swans and geese are large cousins of ducks. Swans are among the heaviest flying birds in North America; many geese commonly feed on grassland and farmland.

TUNDRA SWAN

Most common swan. Breeds in solitary pairs in Arctic tundra; winters in large flocks, mainly in far west and a few places in east. Similar Mute Swan is larger, with more curved neck and orange bill.

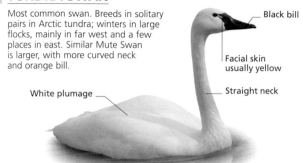

Black bill

Facial skin usually yellow

Straight neck

White plumage

SNOW GOOSE (WHITE FORM)

Breeds in the high Arctic, where many birds pick up rust coloration on the face from feeding in tundra water rich in iron oxide. Winters in large flocks in many parts of the US.

Pink bill

Black outer wing feathers

White body

SNOW GOOSE (BLUE FORM)

The dark color form of Snow Goose, once called "Blue Goose." Has a brown back with pale wing feathers. Most common on Gulf Coast. Similar Ross's Goose has a much smaller bill.

White head

Pink bill with black patch

Dark body

Pink legs

What to look for • Size • Shape • Face pattern • Leg and bill color

CANADA GOOSE

Familiar, widespread, and abundant. Many populations have stopped migrating and the species is now resident in much of the US. Nearly identical Cackling Goose is 25 percent smaller with a much smaller bill.

Black head

Brown back

Black neck

White chin patch

GREATER WHITE-FRONTED GOOSE

Smaller than Canada Goose. Easily distinguished by its black-barred belly and patch of white at base of bill. Breeds in the high Arctic; winters mostly on West Coast and southeastern Great Plains

Pale pink bill with narrow white base

Orange legs

Black bars on belly

BRANT

A small, stocky goose. Western birds have darker bellies than eastern birds. Breeds in the high Arctic; winters in large numbers in saltwater habitats on both coasts.

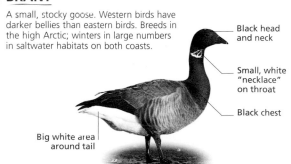

Black head and neck

Small, white "necklace" on throat

Black chest

Big white area around tail

Diving Birds

These highly aquatic birds dive from the surface of the water to pursue their fish prey. All have streamlined bodies, with legs set toward the back of their bodies.

COMMON LOON ☟

Common breeder on large lakes across the northernmost states, Canada, and Alaska. Distinctive far-carrying, yodeling call.

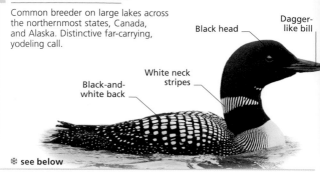

Dagger-like bill

Black head

White neck stripes

Black-and-white back

❋ see below

COMMON LOON ❋

Winters on the ocean on both coasts, as well as on large inland lakes and reservoirs that do not freeze. Sometimes gives distinctive yodeling call in non-breeding season and in flight.

Dagger-like bill

Dark back

Whitish throat

☟ see above

RED-THROATED LOON

Smaller than Common Loon. Breeds on high-Arctic tundra ponds; winters mainly on salt water on both coasts, less commonly on large lakes. Has white face and throat in non-breeding season.

Thin, upturned bill

Gray face

Red throat

Brown back

What to look for • Size • Bill shape
• Neck and throat color

DOUBLE-CRESTED CORMORANT

Most common and widespread
American cormorant; the only
species found inland outside
of Texas, where the Neotropical
Cormorant also occurs. Often
perches on docks and rocks.
Juvenile has pale
breast and neck.

Hook-
tipped
bill

Black body

RED-NECKED GREBE

Smaller, duskier version of Western Grebe. Breeds
on lakes in the north; winters mainly on salt water
on both coasts and eastern Great Lakes. Has dusky
neck and brownish cap in non-breeding plumage.

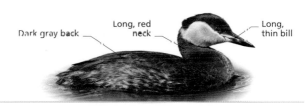

Long, red
neck

Dark gray back

Long,
thin bill

WESTERN GREBE

Same size as Red-throated Loon.
Breeds in large lakes in the west;
winters on west coast and large
interior lakes. Strays found in the
east. Similar Clark's Grebe
has white above eyes.

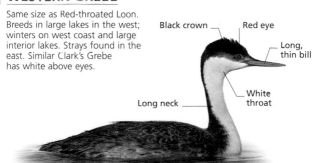

Black crown

Red eye

Long,
thin bill

White
throat

Long neck

Rails

Rails are plump-looking wetland birds. The coot and gallinule are very aquatic, but other rails are shy, secretive inhabitants of dense marsh grasses.

What to look for • Bill size, shape, and color • Body color

AMERICAN COOT

Common and widespread; can be found on almost any body of water, or walking on nearby shoreline. Forms small to large flocks in winter. Juvenile paler than adult.

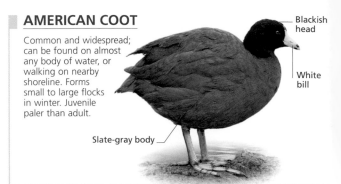

Blackish head

White bill

Slate-gray body

COMMON GALLINULE

Known as Common Moorhen until recently. Resident year-round in freshwater habitats across the southern US. Spreads northward as far as Great Lakes in summer. Juvenile paler than adult, with dull bill.

Slate-gray body

Red bill with yellow tip

White flank streak

VIRGINIA RAIL

Common but secretive; breeds primarily in freshwater marshes. Also found in saltwater marshes, particularly in winter. Similar-looking, widespread Sora has short, yellow bill.

Gray face

Long bill

Chestnut breast and belly

Stocky Water Birds

These birds are always found on or near water. They all have stocky bodies but are unrelated to each other and have very different lifestyles.

What to look out for • Shape • Bill shape • Behavior

PIED-BILLED GREBE

Smaller than Coot. Resident in southern states and on west coast throughout the year. Spreads north to Canada in summer. In winter is browner and lacks black bill mark.

Short, thick bill with black ring

Gray-brown body

Black chin

BELTED KINGFISHER

Widespread, unmistakable bird. Dives head first into water from perch or hovering position to catch fish. Female has rusty band across belly. Loud, distinctive rattle-like call.

Bushy crest

Dagger-like bill

White collar

Slate-blue breastband

DIPPER

Songbird with an unusual feeding technique—swims and walks underwater to feed on aquatic insects. Resident of mountain streams in the west, north to Alaska; winters at lower elevations.

Dark head

Straight, black bill

Slate-gray body

Wading Birds

All these birds wade in shallow water. Cranes have shaggy tails and ibises have curved bills, while herons fly with their necks pulled into an "S" curve.

SANDHILL CRANE

Tall bird of central wetlands and grasslands. Breeds from the northern US to the high Arctic; winters in the south, spreading to the east. Juveniles are browner than adults.

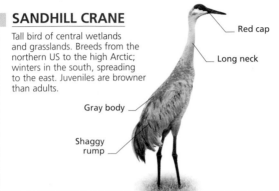

Red cap

Long neck

Gray body

Shaggy rump

GREAT BLUE HERON

The largest American heron, as tall as Sandhill Crane. Widespread and resident over much of the US; breeds north into Canada. Nests in colonies in dead trees.

Black head stripe

Long neck

Shaggy plumes

Slate-gray back

BLACK-CROWNED NIGHT-HERON

Medium-sized, resident of east and west coasts and the Deep South; breeds throughout most of the continent. Young birds are streaked with brown.

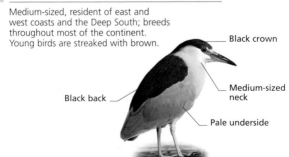

Black crown

Medium-sized neck

Black back

Pale underside

What to look out for • Size • Body color • Bill color and shape • Leg color

GREAT EGRET

Slightly smaller than Great Blue Heron. Resident in the Deep South; moves north to breed. After breeding may occur anywhere in North America.

White body _____

Yellow bill

Black legs

GREEN HERON

Small, dark, and stocky. Prefers wooded, wet areas. Resident of Florida, the West Coast, and the southwest; breeds over most of the eastern US. Most often seen flying away, with a loud squawk.

Greenish back

Short neck

Stocky body

WHITE-FACED IBIS

Same size as Black-crowned Night-Heron. Resident on western Gulf Coast; breeds in western wetlands. Mostly migratory. Glossy Ibis in the east is similar but has dark legs and eyes.

Dark brown body

Long, downcurved bill

Glossy, greenish wings

Reddish legs

Medium Shorebirds

These common, medium-sized birds are found near the shore and largely rely on water for food. The phalarope and the turnstone are slightly larger than the others.

SPOTTED SANDPIPER

Common; breeds over northern coast; winters across south. Distinctive flight: wings quiver while held stiffly with slight downward curve. Juveniles and winter birds have no spots.

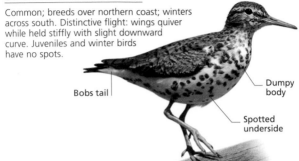

Bobs tail

Dumpy body

Spotted underside

WILSON'S PHALAROPE

Breeds in western interior, eastward to the Great Lakes. Common migrant in the west, uncommon in the east. Juveniles and winter birds have white throats and gray backs.

Small head

Dumpy body

Long, thin bill

RUDDY TURNSTONE

Unmistakable in spring, with a black-and-white head and rusty upperparts. Breeds in the high Arctic; migrant on both coasts and the Great Lakes. Juveniles have a more muted pattern.

Rusty back

Bold face pattern

Black chest

Short, orange legs

What to look for • Bill size and shape • Back color
• Face pattern

DUNLIN ⚥

Widespread; breeds in the high
Arctic; common migrant on both
coasts. Rare to uncommon
inland. In flight, has
a white wing stripe
and a dark rump
and tail center.

Reddish
back

Long,
drooping
bill

Black
underside

✳ see below

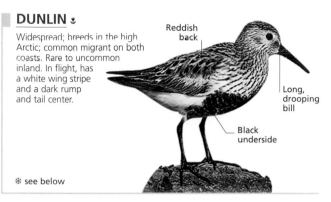

DUNLIN ✳

Common and widespread. Migrates to
the coasts in fall; winters on Atlantic,
Pacific, and Gulf coasts, sometimes in
large flocks. Flight call a
raspy, harsh *kree*.

Long,
drooping
bill

Gray back

White
belly

⚥ see above

SANDERLING

Breeds in the high Arctic; common
in fall and winter on all coasts.
Follows waves back and forth on
sandy beaches. Winter birds
have a gray back and white
face and neck.

Black, reddish,
and white
upperparts

Rust and
black head

Medium-
sized
black bill

Black legs

White
underside

Large & Small Shorebirds

Shorebirds have long legs in proportion to their bodies. These are some of the smallest and largest shorebirds in North America.

LEAST SANDPIPER

North America's smallest sandpiper. Common migrant. Breeds in the Arctic; winters in the southern US. Might be found on wet ground anywhere. Legs can look dark when muddy.

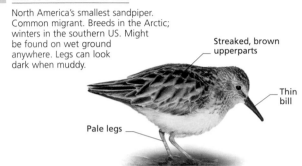

Streaked, brown upperparts

Thin bill

Pale legs

SEMIPALMATED SANDPIPER

Migrates in large numbers over eastern part of the continent. Rare in west south of Canada. Winters in Central and South America. Juveniles and non-breeding adults have much less streaking on breasts.

Gray-brown back

Thick, straight bill

Black legs

MARBLED GODWIT

Breeds on the high prairies; winters on Pacific and Gulf coasts. Uncommon in the east. Cinnamon-colored wing linings visible in flight. Similar Hudsonian Godwit has black wing linings and deep chestnut underparts.

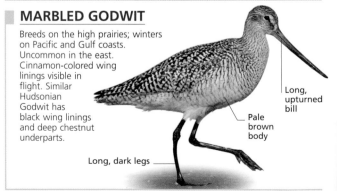

Long, upturned bill

Pale brown body

Long, dark legs

What to look for • Size • Leg length • Bill length • Bill shape

AMERICAN AVOCET

Large and unmistakable. Breeds in shallow-water areas in the west; winters on Pacific and Gulf coasts. Less common in the east, but increasing in numbers. Adults have gray heads in winter.

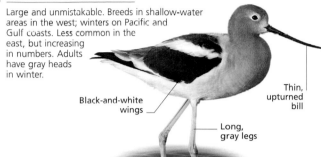

Thin, upturned bill

Black-and-white wings

Long, gray legs

BLACK-NECKED STILT

Smaller than American Avocet, but equally distinctive. Has the longest legs relative to body size of all birds. Breeds in the west and the south. Resident in southern Florida, California, and the Gulf Coast.

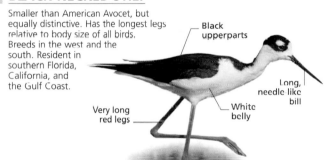

Black upperparts

Long, needle-like bill

White belly

Very long red legs

WHIMBREL

Large migrant. Breeds in tundra region; winters on southern coasts. Flight call a distinctive series of whistles at same pitch. Similar Long-billed Curlew is larger; common in west and on Gulf Coast.

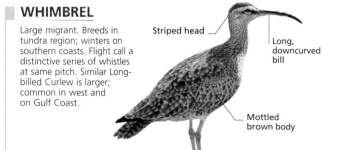

Striped head

Long, downcurved bill

Mottled brown body

Short-billed Shorebirds

These shorebirds have plump bodies and small heads. They are all migrants from their Arctic breeding grounds.

BLACK-BELLIED PLOVER ⬇

Medium-sized and common at coasts. Rare inland, except near Great Lakes. Flight call a distinctive whistled *pee-o-eee*.

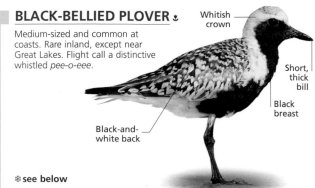

Whitish crown

Short, thick bill

Black breast

Black-and-white back

✳ **see below**

BLACK-BELLIED PLOVER ✳

In winter, this plover has black "armpits" under its wings, which are visible in flight. Juvenile is streaked below. Common on Atlantic, Pacific, and Gulf coasts, where it winters in varying numbers.

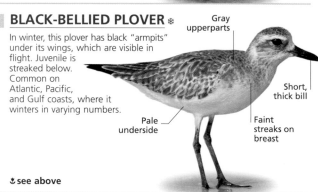

Gray upperparts

Short, thick bill

Faint streaks on breast

Pale underside

⬇ **see above**

RED KNOT ✳

A sandpiper, noticeably smaller than Black-bellied Plover. Rusty breast in breeding plumage, speckled white in winter. Rare migrant inland; regular on coasts. Sometimes forms dense flocks, though its numbers are declining.

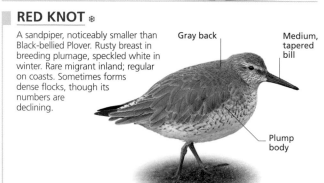

Gray back

Medium, tapered bill

Plump body

What to look for • Color of underparts • Bill size • Overall size

AMERICAN GOLDEN-PLOVER ☙

Slightly smaller than Black-bellied Plover. Favors fields and grasslands, but found on coasts. Migrates mainly through the east; rare in the west. Flight call higher-pitched and sharper than Black-bellied.

Small bill

Mottled golden back

Dark underside

Black feathers under base of tail

❋ see below

AMERICAN GOLDEN-PLOVER ❋

In winter is generally darker than Black-bellied Plover. Easily distinguished from Black-bellied Plover in flight by its dark rump and lack of black "armpits."

Pale eyebrow

Small bill

Brownish back

Dusky underside

☙ see above

SEMIPALMATED PLOVER

Small plover. Common in migration on mudflats and beaches, inland and on coasts. Similar and slightly larger Wilson's Plover on southern coasts has larger, black bill.

Dark brown back

Small bill with orange base

Black band on chest

Yellow legs

Long-billed Shorebirds

These shorebirds use their long bills to feed, often in mud. The Willet and Greater Yellowlegs are bigger than the dowitcher, woodcock, snipe, and sandpiper.

SHORT-BILLED DOWITCHER

Common migrant in the east; breeds in the Arctic. Grayer in winter than in summer. Rapid *tututu* call. Extremely similar Long-billed Dowitcher has higher-pitched *kik*, call sometimes rapid.

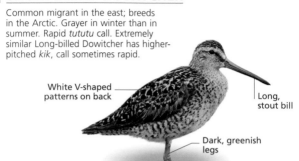

White V-shaped patterns on back

Long, stout bill

Dark, greenish legs

AMERICAN WOODCOCK

Common in the east, strays in the west. Favors wet, wooded areas. Shy, nocturnal; performs elaborate flight displays at dusk. Wings twitter when bird is flushed. Gives buzzy *peent* call in spring.

Barred crown

Short, rounded wings

Long bill, wide at base

WILSON'S SNIPE

Breeds across Canada and the northern US; winters across the southern US. Favors wet fields and grassy shorelines. During display flights, flies up and descends quickly, producing unique, loud, vibrating sound.

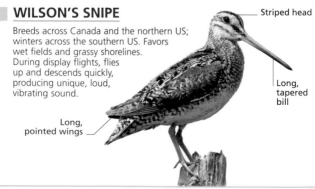

Striped head

Long, tapered bill

Long, pointed wings

What to look for • Size • Wing pattern • Pattern of rump and tail in flight • Leg color

WILLET

Common on coast; uncommon inland Nests in salt- and freshwater marshes. Plain gray in winter. Distinctive, territorial, *pill-will-willet* call.

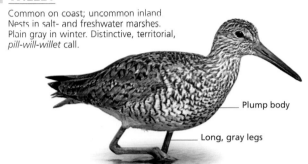

Plump body

Long, gray legs

GREATER YELLOWLEGS

Common migrant, breeds in the Arctic; winters on coast and in the south. Loud *kew, kew, kew* call. Lesser Yellowlegs is very similar but smaller.

Faint eye-ring

Long, thin bill

Streaked neck

Long, yellow legs

SOLITARY SANDPIPER

Smaller and darker than Greater Yellowlegs, with more prominent eye-ring. Nests in Canadian forests; migrants found in wetlands across the continent. Barred tail and dark rump are obvious in flight.

Prominent eye-ring

Dark brown, spotted back

Bobs tail

Olive legs

COMMON MURRE
p.100

COMMON TERN
p.98

AMERICAN OYSTERCATCHER
p.102

Cliffs

Cliffs provide secure nesting places for birds that live at sea, such as murres and kittiwakes. They also shelter nesting land birds such as Peregrine Falcons (p.59) from disturbance and predators.

Sandy shore

Sand and pebbles are easily swept or blown away, and make difficult places for tiny animals to live. This means that only a few birds feed on sandy shores, but many gulls, terns, and plovers nest on open beaches.

5 COAST & SEA

The sea enriches coastal habitats in the same way that freshwater adds variety to the land. Even urban seaside areas have birds—many can be seen in coastal towns and harbors. However, it is less disturbed areas such as muddy shores and cliffs that are really remarkable for birds.

Estuaries

Occuring where rivers meet the sea, estuaries are a mix of fresh and salt water. They are rich and varied places—tides cover and expose mud and silt twice a day, bringing nutrients for the invertebrates that live there, and creating opportunities for birds to feed on them.

GREATER YELLOWLEGS
p.89

SOOTY SHEARWATER
p.102

NORTHERN GANNET
p.95

WILSON'S STORM-PETREL
p.101

At sea

Seabirds are wonderfully adapted to a tough ocean life. They can be seen flying past promontories, especially during gales, but to see them truly at home in this demanding environment it is best to get out in a boat.

BRANT
p.75

Muddy shore

The weighty stability of mud and the rich nutrients brought in by the tides mean that muddy shores, creeks, and estuaries are much better for most birds than sand. However, at high tide birds need to find safe refuge elsewhere.

RED KNOT
Winter, p.86

Medium & Large Gulls

These gulls have white heads during the breeding season; some have streaked heads in the winter. Juvenile gulls take two to four years to acquire adult plumage.

HERRING GULL

Resident in the Great Lakes and mid-Atlantic states northward. Breeds across northern Canada; winters in eastern US and on both east and west coasts. Adult has streaked head in winter.

Pale gray back

Yellow bill

Pink legs

RING-BILLED GULL

Smaller than Herring Gull. Widespread, most common gull inland. Breeds in the north; winters in most of the US. Back of head is streaked in winter.

Yellow bill with black ring

Pale gray back

Yellow legs

CALIFORNIA GULL

Smaller than Herring Gull but slightly larger than Ring-billed Gull. Streaked head in winter. Breeds in freshwater habitats in the west; winters mainly in far west. Rare on Atlantic and Gulf coasts.

Yellow bill with red and black spots

Gray back

Greenish yellow legs

What to look for • Overall size • Back and leg color
• Bill size and markings

GLAUCOUS GULL

Large, pale bird. Breeds in the high
Arctic; winters along the Canadian
and New England coasts and the
Great Lakes. Uncommon to rare
south to Gulf Coast. Very similar
Iceland Gull in the
east is smaller.

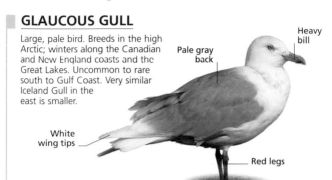

Heavy
bill

Pale gray
back

White
wing tips

Red legs

GREAT BLACK-BACKED GULL

Largest North American gull. Resident on the
coast from Virginia to the Maritime Provinces
and in eastern Great Lakes; strays westward.
Similar Lesser Black-backed Gull is
smaller, with yellow legs.

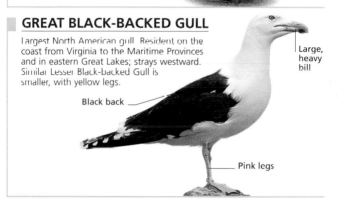

Large,
heavy
bill

Black back

Pink legs

WESTERN GULL

Similar size to Herring Gull. Common
resident on West Coast of the US;
rare away from coast. Birds from
southern part of range
have darker backs than
northern birds.

Large bill

Slate-gray
back

Pink legs

Small Gulls & Gull-like Birds

These relatively small gulls usually breed inland and winter along the coast. The Kittiwake, Fulmar, and Gannet nest on sea cliffs and winter mainly at sea.

FRANKLIN'S GULL

Small gull; partial black hood in winter adults and juveniles. Breeds in north-central interior and parts of the west; migrates through central region; rare on both coasts.

Slate-gray back

Black-and-white wing tips

Black hood on summer adults

Prominent white eye crescents

Pinkish underparts

LAUGHING GULL

Larger than Franklin's Gull with less prominent eye crescents. Winter adults and juveniles lack hood. Resident in Gulf and southeast coasts; breeds as far as Canada; rare inland except at the Salton Sea.

Black hood on summer adults

Slate-gray back

Black wing tips

Long legs

BONAPARTE'S GULL

Smaller than Franklin's Gull. Black hood in breeding season. Breeds in far north; migrant through most of continent. Winters on Great Lakes and along the coasts, especially southeast.

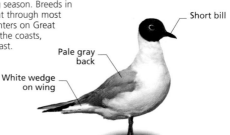

Short bill

Pale gray back

White wedge on wing

What to look for • Size • Wing pattern • Shape
• Bill size

BLACK-LEGGED KITTIWAKE

Medium-sized gull. Winter adults
have black smudge behind eye;
juveniles have black bars on
wings and black on back of
neck. Sometimes seen from
shore, especially in west; rare
migrant inland.

Small,
yellow
bill

Pale gray
back

Black wing tips

NORTHERN FULMAR

Larger than Kittiwake. Very
stiff-winged in flight. Very
seen from shore except near breeding
cliffs. Dark gray form more
common in north.

Tubes on
upper
bill

Gray back

Paddle-like
wings

NORTHERN GANNET

Often seen from shore. In
non-breeding season, seen off
Atlantic and Gulf coasts. Dives
headfirst from considerable
height into water to catch fish.
Immatures have dark or blotchy
white plumage.

Golden
head

Long,
gray
bill

Long,
thin
wings

Black outer
wing feathers

Gulls

Gulls take two to four years to mature fully. As they get older their plumage changes, making it possible to tell the ages of different individuals.

Changes in plumage come about when birds molt—old feathers fall out and are replaced with new ones. Most juvenile gulls are brown and become pale gray, white, and black with age. Adult gulls alternate between breeding (summer) and non-breeding (winter) plumage—look for changes in spring and late summer/fall. The birds shown here are all Herring Gulls.

Blackish bill

Sharp, black wingtips with white spots

Dark bars on back

Black wingtips and tail band

First winter

A gull's first feathers are its brownish juvenile plumage. In its first fall, a gull molts into its first winter plumage. It molts again in spring into its first summer plumage. The bill remains almost black.

Yellow-and-black bill

Extensive gray on wings and back

White underparts

Third winter

In the second and third years all feathers molt each fall, and head and body feathers molt again each spring, making the young gull look more like an adult.

Summer adult

After four years it is impossible to tell a Herring Gull's precise age by its plumage. However, breeding and non-breeding plumages alternate by season. In summer, an adult gull has a pure white head and bright bill and leg colors.

Pale eye with orange ring

Bright yellow bill with red spot

White chest and head

Gray back and wings

Eye-ring less orange than in summer

Heavily streaked head and breast

Winter adult

In the winter, adult Herring Gulls have brown-streaked heads. The streaked head and breast return to white in spring.

Body same as in summer

Terns

Terns are related to gulls, but are more streamlined and smaller. Their bills are usually longer and more pointed, as are their wings. Most adults have black caps.

COMMON TERN

Widespread. Breeds in colonies on Atlantic coast and northern interior, east of Rockies. Migrant; winters in South America. Juveniles and winter adults have dark bar on wings and a white forehead. Dark wedge on outer wing feathers is visible in flight.

Gray back

Red bill with black tip

Red legs

FORSTER'S TERN

Similar size to Common Tern. Breeds in fresh- and saltwater marshes across the continent. Winters in the Gulf and on southeastern coasts. Juveniles and winter adults have a black ear patch and pale crown.

Orange-red bill

Pale gray back

Long outer tail

Red legs

CASPIAN TERN

World's largest tern; as big as a medium-sized gull. Streaked cap in winter. Nests mainly in inland wetlands; winters on the southern coasts.

Large red bill

Dark outer wing feathers

Black legs

What to look for • Size • Bill and leg color • Tail length

SANDWICH TERN

Medium-sized tern of southeastern and Gulf coasts; uncommon in southern California. Juveniles and winter adults have white foreheads and streaked, partial caps.

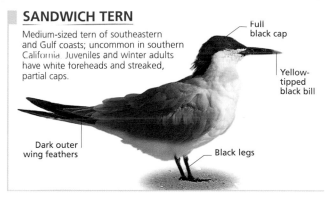

Full black cap

Yellow-tipped black bill

Dark outer wing feathers

Black legs

LEAST TERN

Smallest tern; less than two-thirds the size of Caspian Tern. Breeds in open sandy areas and on rooftops. Rarely spotted outside colonies. Juveniles and winter adults have black bills.

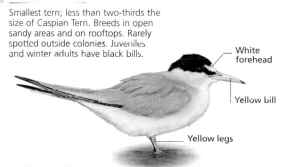

White forehead

Yellow bill

Yellow legs

BLACK TERN

Slightly larger than Least Tern. Breeds on inland marshes and wetlands. Rare on the West Coast. Winter adults and juveniles have white undersides.

Dark gray back; brown on juveniles

Black bill

Gray tail

Black legs

Specialist Seabirds

These birds are found at sea or just offshore, but come to land to breed. The storm-petrel breeds in Antarctica, the others mainly breed in cold, northern waters.

COMMON MURRE

Penguin-like; larger than puffin. Breeds in cliffs on Atlantic and Pacific coasts; winters offshore. Winter adults and juveniles have white throats. Similar Thick-billed Murre has stouter bill with white line.

Tapering, pointed bill

Sooty gray upperparts

White underside

ATLANTIC PUFFIN

Smallest puffin. Breeds in Maine and northward; winters at sea. Winter adult and juvenile have dusky cheeks; juvenile also has smaller bill. Horned Puffin in Pacific has red and yellow bill.

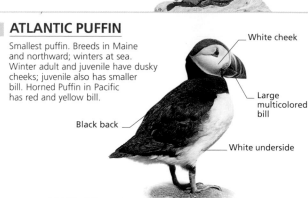

White cheek

Large multicolored bill

Black back

White underside

TUFTED PUFFIN

Largest puffin, found only on the Pacific coast. Winter adult has dark face, mainly red bill, and only a trace of the tufts. Juvenile is similar to winter adult, but generally has smaller bill.

White face

Large red and yellow bill

Black body

What to look for • Size • Bill size and shape • Bill color
• Face pattern

RHINOCEROS AUKLET

Slightly smaller than Tufted Puffin. Breeds
along the northern Pacific coast; winters
on the southern coast to Baja California.
Juvenile and winter adult lack "rhino"
horn and tufts.

Two white facial tufts

"Rhino" horn on top of bill

Yellow bill

MARBLED MURRELET

Smaller than Rhinoceros Auklet. Breeds
high in trees in northern California and
northward to Alaska; winters on coast in
the same area. Winter bird black above,
white below, with white collar.

Dark upperparts

Mottled brown underside

Short, thin bill

Short neck

WILSON'S STORM-PETREL

Small seabird. Common in the Atlantic
in summer, sometimes close to the
shore. Feeding birds "dance" over
the water.

Dark back

Small, black "tube nose"

White rump

Coastal & Ocean Birds

These seabirds are fairly distinctive. The pelican and the oystercatcher are coastal birds, but shearwaters usually stay out at sea.

What to look for • Size • Shape • Bill shape and size

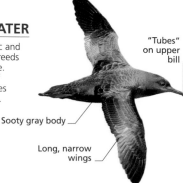

SOOTY SHEARWATER

Found on ocean off Atlantic and Pacific coasts in summer; breeds in the Southern Hemisphere. Flight marked by rapid, stiff wingbeats and soaring glides close to the water's surface.

"Tubes" on upper bill

Sooty gray body

Long, narrow wings

BROWN PELICAN

Very large. Resident in southern California and Gulf and south-eastern coasts; post-breeding birds wander northward. Larger White Pelican breeds inland; winters in southern areas.

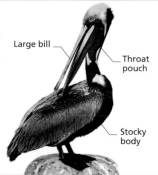

Large bill

Throat pouch

Stocky body

AMERICAN OYSTERCATCHER

Large and distinctive, with black head and contrasting red bill. Resident in mid-Atlantic to Gulf coasts; breeds north to Canada. Uncommon in southern California. Similar Black Oystercatcher is restricted to Pacific Coast.

Black head and breast

Brown back

Large, red bill

White belly

BIRD GALLERY

This color gallery shows the birds already profiled in the book, but grouped by color. When you see a bird, flick through the color groupings to find options most like the bird you are watching, then go to their profile page for a closer look. Some birds appear in more than one color grouping.

Size guide

Birds are grouped in four sizes. Apparent size is more a function of "bulk" than length, so these groups are not precise—but they can help you figure out what you are looking at.

COLOR GROUP

TINY (House Sparrow)   SMALL (Rock Pigeon)

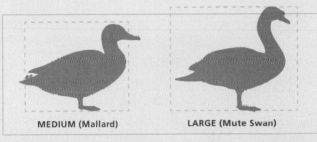

MEDIUM (Mallard)   LARGE (Mute Swan)

Contents

WHITE

Tundra Swan
p.74

Great Egret
p.81

GRAY

Brown
Pelican
p.102

Great Blue
Heron
p.80

Common Gallinule
p.78

Rhinoceros Auklet
p.101

Rock Pigeon
p.27

Brown-headed Cowbird ♀
p.19

Dark-eyed Junco
p.21

Tufted Titmouse
p.23

GRAY BACKS

Common Merganser ♀
p.71

Dunlin ✳
p.83

Northern Gannet
p.95

Snow Goose (White Form)
p.74

Sandhill Crane
p.80

Gadwall ♂
p.64

American Coot
p.78

Northern Mockingbird
p.22

Gray Catbird
p.22

Dipper
p.79

Bushtit
p.42

Blue-gray Gnatcatcher
p.42

American Pipit
p.54

STREAKED GRAY BACKS

Northern Pintail ♂
p.65

Redhead ♂
p.68

Wilson's Phalarope
p.82

Solitary Sandpiper
p.89

Eastern Whip-poor-will
p.35

GRAY-BLUE BACKS

Peregrine Falcon
p.59

Cooper's Hawk
p.58

Belted Kingfisher
p.79

Blue Jay
p.26

Eastern Bluebird
p.41

White-breasted Nuthatch
p.43

Indigo Bunting
p.41

Blue-gray Gnatcatcher
p.42

Green-winged Teal ♂
p.65

Greater Yellowlegs
p.89

Black-bellied Plover ♣
p.86

Common Nighthawk
p.35

Red-bellied
Woodpecker
p.24

White-tailed Kite
p.58

Rock Pigeon
p.27

Merlin
p.59

Blue Grosbeak
p.41

Barn Swallow
p.29

Tree Swallow
p.29

GRAY AND WHITE

Common Loon ✳
p.76

Glaucous Gull
p.93

California Gull
p.92

Red-necked Grebe
p.77

Northern Fulmar
p.95

GRAY, BLACK, AND WHITE

Black-crowned Night-Heron
p.80

Caspian Tern
p.98

Franklin's Gull
p.94

Sandwich Tern
p.99

Common Tern
p.98

Least Tern
p.99

Loggerhead Shrike
p.53

White-breasted Nuthatch
p.43

Red-throated Loon
p.76

Herring Gull
p.92

Western Gull
p.93

Ring-billed Gull
p.92

Black-legged Kittiwake
p.95

Northern Harrier
p.58

Lesser Scaup ♂
p.68

Laughing Gull
p.94

White-tailed Kite
p.58

Forster's Tern
p.98

Bonaparte's Gull
p.94

Black-bellied Plover ⚥
p.86

BLACK AND WHITE

Bald Eagle
p.56

Northern Gannet
p.95

Osprey
p.56

Brant
p.75

Western Grebe
p.77

Common Murre
p.100

Pileated Woodpecker
p.37

Black-billed Magpie
p.26

Bufflehead ♀
p.71

Atlantic Puffin
p.100

Red-headed Woodpecker
p.37

Bobolink
p.55

Black-and-white Warbler
p.43

Black-capped Chickadee
p.23

Common Loon ⚓
p.76

Great Black-backed Gull
p.93

Snow Goose (White Form)
p.74

Common Merganser ♂
p.69

American Oystercatcher
p.102

American Avocet
p.85

Tufted Puffin
p.100

Black-necked Stilt
p.85

Bufflehead ♂
p.69

Yellow-bellied
Sapsucker
p.37

Eastern Kingbird
p.39

Downy Woodpecker
p.24

BLACK

Double-crested Cormorant
p.77

Turkey Vulture
p.56

Black Tern
p.99

Red-winged Blackbird ♂
p.18

European Starling
p.18

PLAIN BROWN BACKS

White-faced Ibis
p.81

Mallard ♂
p.64

Mourning Dove
p.27

Yellow-billed Cuckoo
p.27

Brown Thrasher
p.22

Swainson's Thrush
p.40

Hermit Thrush
p.40

Chimney Swift
p.29

Sooty Shearwater
p.102

American Crow
p.26

Common Grackle
p.19

Brown-headed Cowbird ♂
p.19

Wilson's Storm-Petrel
p.101

Ruddy Duck ♂
p.69

Ruddy Duck ♀
p.71

Pied-billed Grebe
p.79

Killdeer
p.50

Semipalmated Plover
p.87

Veery
p.40

MOTTLED BROWN BACKS

Red-tailed Hawk
p.57

Swainson's Hawk
p.57

Northern Shoveler ♀
p.70

American Wigeon ♀
p.67

Redhead ♀
p.70

Broad-winged Hawk
p.57

Lesser Scaup ♀
p.70

Willet
p.89

American Golden-Plover ✿
p.87

Marbled Murrelet
p.101

Ruddy Turnstone
p.82

Semipalmated Sandpiper
p.84

Least Sandpiper
p.84

Mallard ♀
p.66

Gadwall ♀
p.66

Northern Pintail ♀
p.67

Wood Duck ♀
p.66

Marbled Godwit
p.84

Whimbrel
p.85

Green-winged Teal ♀
p.67

Red Knot ❀
p.86

American Golden Plover ☙
p.87

Western Meadowlark
p.55

Black-headed Grosbeak
p.31

Sanderling ❀
p.83

SMALL, WITH STREAKED OR BARRED BROWN BACKS

American Kestrel
p.59

Marbled Murrelet
p.101

Red-winged Blackbird ♀
p.18

Dunlin ⚥
p.83

Spotted Sandpiper
p.82

Snow Bunting
p.54

Lark Sparrow
p.53

Song Sparrow
p.20

Chipping Sparrow
p.53

Brown Creeper
p.43

House Wren
p.23

RED OR ORANGE

Northern Cardinal
p.25

Baltimore Oriole
p.30

Burrowing Owl
p.51

Virginia Rail
p.78

Eastern Screech-Owl
p.34

Horned Lark
p.54

Northern Pygmy-Owl
p.35

White-throated Sparrow
p.20

House Sparrow
p.20

Dickcissel
p.52

House Finch
p.21

Summer Tanager
p.25

Scarlet Tanager
p.25

American Redstart
p.47

LARGE, WITH STREAKED OR BARRED BROWN BACKS

Wild Turkey
p.36

Canada Goose
p.75

Greater Roadrunner
p.50

Great Horned Owl
p.34

Barred Owl
p.34

Northern Bobwhite
p.36

Northern Flicker
p.24

Upland Sandpiper
p.50

REDDISH UNDERNEATH

Northern Shoveler ♂
p.68

Wood Duck ♂
p.64

Eastern Towhee
p.30

Say's Phoebe
p.52

House Finch
p.21

Snow Goose (Blue Form)
p.74

Greater White-fronted Goose
p.75

Greater Sage-Grouse
p.51

American Wigeon ♂
p.65

Ruffed Grouse
p.36

Short-eared Owl
p.51

Short-billed Dowitcher
p.88

American Woodcock
p.88

Wilson's Snipe
p.88

American Robin
p.30

Black-headed Grosbeak
p.31

Rose-breasted Grosbeak
p.31

Rufous Hummingbird
p.28

Ruby-throated
Hummingbird ♂
p.28

GREENISH BACKS

Green Heron
p.81

Eastern Phoebe
p.38

Northern Waterthrush
p.45

Warbling Vireo
p.44

Least Flycatcher
p.38

Ruby-throated
Hummingbird ♂
p.28

Ruby-throated
Hummingbird ♀
p.28

YELLOWISH UNDERNEATH

Great Crested Flycatcher
p.39

Cedar Waxwing
p.39

Dickcissel
p.52

Yellow Warbler
p.46

American Goldfinch
p.21

Blue-winged Warbler
p.46

Eastern Wood-Pewee
p.38

Red-eyed Vireo
p.44

Ovenbird
p.45

Blue-headed Vireo
p.44

Orange-crowned Warbler
p.45

Golden-crowned Kinglet
p.42

Western Meadowlark
p.55

Yellow-headed Blackbird
p.55

Western Kingbird
p.52

Yellow-rumped Warbler
p.47

Magnolia Warbler
p.47

Common Yellowthroat
p.31

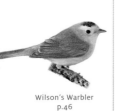

Wilson's Warbler
p.46

Scientific Names

Every living species has a scientific name of two Latin words. The first word is the genus, shared by closely related species which often look similar. The second is the specific name. Each two-word combination is unique to the individual species.

Common name	Scientific name	Page
European Starling	*Sturnus vulgaris*	18
Red-winged Blackbird	*Agelaius pheoniceus*	18
Common Grackle	*Quiscalus quiscala*	19
Brown-headed Cowbird	*Molothrus ater*	19
House Sparrow	*Passer domesticus*	20
Song Sparrow	*Melospiza melodia*	20
White-throated Sparrow	*Zonotrichia albicollis*	20
Dark-eyed Junco	*Junco hyemalis*	21
House Finch	*Carpodacus mexicanus*	21
American Goldfinch	*Spinus tristis*	21
Northern Mockingbird	*Mimus polyglottos*	22
Gray Catbird	*Dumetella carolinensis*	22
Brown Thrasher	*Toxostoma rufum*	22
House Wren	*Troglogytes aedon*	23
Black-capped Chickadee	*Poecile atricapillus*	23
Tufted Titmouse	*Baeolophus bicolor*	23
Downy Woodpecker	*Picoides pubescens*	24
Red-bellied Woodpecker	*Melanerpes carolinus*	24
Northern Flicker	*Colaptes auratus*	24
Northern Cardinal	*Cardinalis cardinalis*	25
Summer Tanager	*Piranga ruber*	25
Scarlet Tanager	*Piranga olivacea*	25
Blue Jay	*Cyanocitta cristata*	26
American Crow	*Corvus brachyrhynchos*	26
Black-billed Magpie	*Pica hudsonia*	26
Rock Pigeon	*Columba livia*	27
Mourning Dove	*Zenaida macroura*	27
Yellow-billed Cuckoo	*Coccyzus americanus*	27
Ruby-throated Hummingbird	*Archilochus colubris*	28
Rufous Hummingbird	*Selasphorus rufus*	28
Chimney Swift	*Chaetura pelagica*	29
Barn Swallow	*Hirundo rustica*	29
Tree Swallow	*Tachycineta bicolor*	29
American Robin	*Turdus migratorius*	30
Baltimore Oriole	*Icterus galbula*	30
Eastern Towhee	*Pipilo erythrophthalmus*	30
Rose-breasted Grosbeak	*Pheucticus ludovicianus*	31
Black-headed Grosbeak	*Pheucticus melanocephalus*	31
Common Yellowthroat	*Geothlypis trichas*	31
Great Horned Owl	*Bubo virginianus*	34
Barred Owl	*Strix varia*	34
Eastern Screech-Owl	*Megascops asio*	34
Northern Pygmy-Owl	*Galucidium gnoma*	35
Common Nighthawk	*Chordeiles minor*	35
Eastern Whip-poor-will	*Caprimulgus vociferus*	35
Ruffed Grouse	*Bonasa umbellus*	36
Northern Bobwhite	*Colinus virginianus*	36
Wild Turkey	*Meleagris gallopavo*	36
Red-headed Woodpecker	*Melanerpes erythrocephalus*	37
Yellow-bellied Sapsucker	*Sphyrapicus varius*	37
Pileated Woodpecker	*Dryocopus pileatus*	37
Eastern Phoebe	*Sayornis phoebe*	38
Eastern Wood-Pewee	*Contopus virens*	38
Least Flycatcher	*Empidonax minimus*	38
Eastern Kingbird	*Tyrannus tyrannus*	39
Great Crested Flycatcher	*Myiarchus crinitus*	39
Cedar Waxwing	*Bombycilla cedrorum*	39

Glossary

Birding has its own jargon, but you actually need to learn very little, and very few new words. Some terms can help you understand birds better and describe them with greater precision. Many parts of birds used in descriptions are shown on p.14.

Bird of prey Bird that preys on other birds or other animals.

Birding The hobby of finding, listing, listening to, and watching birds for enjoyment.

Breeding plumage Plumage worn by adults at the time of mating—sometimes called "summer plumage" but can also occur in winter.

Call (or call note) Short notes used by birds to keep in touch (see song).

Cap/crown A patch of color on top of the head.

Cocked Held upward at an angle, as in a cocked tail.

Covert One of a patch or row of smaller feathers overlying the base of large wing or tail feathers.

Eclipse Dull, female-like plumage assumed by male ducks in summer.

Eye-ring A ring of color, of either fleshy skin or feathers, around the eye.

Eye-stripe or eye-line A line of color through the eye, above the cheeks.

Habitat The type of environment a species lives in, providing food, resting sites, and in summer, nest sites.

Immature A bird that is not yet fully sexually mature. Usually has a different plumage pattern from that of the adult of the species.

Introduced A species or population of birds brought by humans to a geographic area where it did not occur naturally.

Listing Keeping lists of the birds seen in different areas.

Migrant A bird that moves between different geographical areas at different times of the year.

Molt The regular process of shedding and replacing feathers.

Mustache A stripe of color from the bill, beneath the cheek.

Native Naturally occurring in an area; not introduced by people.

Ornithology The scientific study of birds.

Plumage The covering of feathers. Also various overall patterns or colors that identify different ages, sexes, and seasonal changes in a bird's appearance.

Resident Found year-round in a specific area.

Roost To roost (to sleep), or a roost (a place where birds spend the night, or rest during non-feeding periods such as high tide).

Sally To fly out from a perch to catch prey, then return to perch or nearby.

Shorebird A shoreline bird: especially a plover, sandpiper, or allied species.

Song A particular type of vocal performance that identifies a species, used mostly (but not always) by males, to advertise their presence to others.

Species A "type" of bird, individuals of which can interbreed and produce fertile, viable young; hybrids between species are generally infertile.

Strays Bird occurring far outside its normal range.

Vagrant See Strays.

Wader In America, usually refers to the larger, long-legged birds of the shore and wetlands, such as herons and ibis. In Britain, refers to shorebirds (above).

Index

Page numbers in **bold** indicate main entry.

Acknowledgments

Dorling Kindersley would like to thank: Rob Hume for initial guidance; David Roberts for database support; Claire Bowers and Susie Peachey, DK Picture Library; Jamie Ambrose for editorial; Vritti Bansal for design; Oliver Metcalf for content suggestions; and Jill Hamilton for proofreading.

The publisher would also like to thank the following for their kind permission to reproduce their photographs:

(**Key:** a-above; b-below/bottom; c-center; f-far; l-left; r-right; t-top)

4 Alamy Images: Arco Images GmbH (br). **6-7 Getty Images:** Susan Gary. **9 Robert Royse:** (tl). **14 FLPA:** Franz Christoph Robi / Imagebroker (bc). **15 Corbis:** Glenn Bartley / All Canada Photos. **16-17 Corbis:** Paul Thompson. **29 Christopher Taylor:** (tc). **54 Robert Royse:** (bc). **59 Dreamstime.com:** Chris Lorenz (c). **62-63 naturepl.com:** Peter Cairns. **62 Robert Royse:** (br). **66 Markus Varesvuo:** (bc). **67 Melvin Grey:** (bc). **69 Robert Royse:** (bc). **70 Markus Varesvuo:** (ca). **71 Melvin Grey:** (c). **Robert Royse:** (bc, br). **73 Robert Royse:** (br). **76 Robert Royse:** (bc). **80 Robert Royse:** (bc). **87 Robert Royse:** (bc). **90-91 Getty Images:** Anthony Thomas. **91 Robert Royse:** (tl). **96 Richard Ford / digitalwildlife.co.uk:** (bc). **101 Robert Royse:** (bc). **103 Alamy Images:** Arco Images GmbH (br). **104 Melvin Grey:** (bc). **107 Dreamstime.com:** Chris Lorenz (cr). **108 Robert Royse:** (c). **112 Christopher Taylor:** (br). **113 Robert Royse:** (ca, cb, clb, bc). **114 Robert Royse:** (clb). **Markus Varesvuo:** (cla). **115 Melvin Grey:** (tr). **Markus Varesvuo:** (tc). **116 Robert Royse:** (cl)

All other images © Dorling Kindersley. For further information see: **www.dkimages.com**